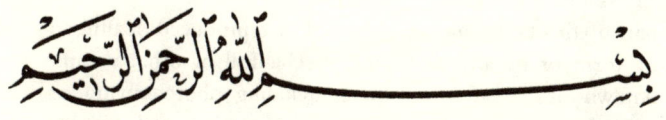

© Abdussabur Kirke 2020

No part of this book may be reprinted or reproduced or utilised in any form or by any electronic, mechanical or other means, not known or hereafter invented, including photocopying or recording, or in any information storage or retrieval system, without permission in writing from the publisher.

Abdussabur Kirke asserts the moral right to be identified as the author of this work.

Jacket photograph: Aziz Kirke
Cover calligraphy: Aisha Wright

All rights reserved

Lifeboat Press
info@lifeboatpress.org

ISBN: 978-0-620-88069-5
Manufactured in the United Kingdom

THE GARDEN OF PRESENCE

Abdussabur Kirke

LIFEBOAT PRESS

CONTENTS

The Presence of the Hour 7
Truth and the Prayer 17
The Transmission of the Sunna 27
Leadership, Work, Helping People 37
The Emergence of Meaning 45
Future Uncertainty 55
Justice of the Decree and Free Will 69
Language and Knowledge 83
Riba and Madness 95
Technology and the Environment 103
The Garden of Presence 115

THE PRESENCE OF THE HOUR

Death, like the Hour, is ever-present, since with every life-giving contraction of the heart – the systole – comes the diastole, the lull, in which the flow stops. If this is extended, it is death, a death annulled only by the next beat.

All creation is suspended in this state between life and death at every moment. It dies in every instant, but Allah, the Living and the Self-Sustaining, keeps it alive and bursting with vigour, strength and will, until death arrives.

It is the same with the Hour, which is ever-present but expunged by Allah's continued sustenance of time and space. The moment those are removed, time and space are over.

Knowledge of this cannot be acquired in the conventional sense, because the instrument of conventional knowledge exists only in time and space. But the heart can perceive it.

Allah, subhanahu wa ta'ala, says in Surat Ahzab:

يَسْـَٔلُكَ ٱلنَّاسُ عَنِ ٱلسَّاعَةِ ۖ قُلْ إِنَّمَا عِلْمُهَا عِندَ ٱللَّهِ ۚ وَمَا يُدْرِيكَ لَعَلَّ ٱلسَّاعَةَ تَكُونُ قَرِيبًا ۝

People will ask you about the Last Hour.
Say: 'Only Allah has knowledge of it.
What will make you understand?
It may be that the Last Hour is very near.'

Elsewhere He, subhanahu wa ta'ala, instructs us not to speculate on its date:

يَسْـَٔلُونَكَ عَنِ ٱلسَّاعَةِ أَيَّانَ مُرْسَىٰهَا ۝ فِيمَ أَنتَ مِن ذِكْرَىٰهَا ۝ إِلَىٰ رَبِّكَ مُنتَهَىٰهَا ۝

They ask you about the Hour:
'When will it come?'
What are you doing mentioning it?
Its coming is your Lord's affair.

Speculating on the coming of the Hour leads to a paralysis that can be seen in certain groups who define their activities in terms of waiting and preparing for either the Last Day or some coming prelude to it, like the Mahdi. What this means is total political capitulation.

Notwithstanding, the Hour is mentioned dozens of times in the Qur'an and further times still in the Hadith, so it is an important element of our understanding.

In Surat al-'Araf He says, subhanahu wa ta'ala:

$$ثَقُلَتْ فِى السَّمَوَاتِ وَالْأَرْضِ$$

It hangs heavy in the heavens and the earth.

And in Surat an-Nahl:

$$وَمَآ أَمْرُ السَّاعَةِ إِلَّا كَلَمْحِ الْبَصَرِ أَوْ هُوَ أَقْرَبُ$$

The matter of the Hour
is only the blink of an eye away,
or even nearer.

So while there is certainly a chronological dimension to this final historical event – it will come – there is another dimension to its nearness.

The Last Hour is present in every moment. Not that this denies its coming in time. But it is nevertheless built into every moment, just as death is present in every moment.

* * *

These are the secrets which we seek especially in the nights of Ramadan, alone or in the jama'at of Tarawih.

Allah, subhanahu wa ta'ala, uses the same word, 'qareeb', in Surat al-Waqi'a to describe His own presence, subhanahu wa ta'ala, at the moment of death:

$$\text{وَنَحْنُ أَقْرَبُ إِلَيْهِ مِنكُمْ وَلَٰكِن لَّا تُبْصِرُونَ}$$

and We are nearer him than you but you cannot see –

And in Surat Qaf:

$$\text{وَنَحْنُ أَقْرَبُ إِلَيْهِ مِنْ حَبْلِ ٱلْوَرِيدِ}$$

We are nearer to him than his jugular vein.

The jugular vein is the channel of our life-blood, as near to our sense of self as we can get, yet He is nearer than that. He is nearer to us than ourselves.

These are the gifts of Ramadan, because Ramadan is the breaking of norms and withdrawal from habits. Ramadan isn't *not eating*. It is eating at a different time from usual. It is sleeping at different times from usual. It reveals our habits and patterns.

The prayer does the same for us, but in the realm of time. It demands to be done in its time, and if not, then it bears on us to make it up, so we have to put aside other things – and in doing so, we see them for what they are.

The Zakat is like that for wealth. It demands the relinquishing not of a significant amount of money, but of the illusion that we are the sole custodians of our wealth and its controllers.

Hajj is laying down life itself, as you go not knowing you will definitely return, and often at great cost to wealth and even health, and you go dressed in your burial clothes.

The Shahada demands that you accept knowledge that is not from you. It is given to you by the Best of Creation, Al-Amin, the Trustworthy, the Messenger of Allah, sallallahu 'alayhi wa sallam, who was never untruthful. And at the same time, we *recognise* that knowledge when it comes to us, especially if we have realised that our own knowledge is not enough. Allah ta'ala says in Surat al-Balad:

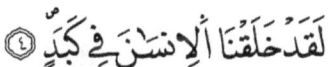

We created man in trouble.

In other words, it is normal that we are troubled, and we are in ourselves not living, not knowing, and the creation itself is over in every instant – except, by the Mercy of Allah, we find ourselves alright, things are working out, we are alive, the natural world continues to run on its extraordinary pattern, full of possibilities for us.

Allah, subhanahu ta'ala, says in Surat az-Zumar:

$$\text{وَإِن تَشْكُرُوا يَرْضَهُ لَكُمْ}$$

But if you are grateful,
He is pleased with you for that.

The 27th Night of Ramadan is often considered most likely to be the Laylatul-Qadr, the Night of Power. Allah, subhanahu wa ta'ala, says:

$$\text{إِنَّا أَنزَلْنَاهُ فِي لَيْلَةِ الْقَدْرِ ۝ وَمَا أَدْرَاكَ مَا لَيْلَةُ الْقَدْرِ ۝ لَيْلَةُ الْقَدْرِ خَيْرٌ مِّنْ أَلْفِ شَهْرٍ ۝ تَنَزَّلُ الْمَلَائِكَةُ وَالرُّوحُ فِيهَا بِإِذْنِ رَبِّهِم مِّن كُلِّ أَمْرٍ ۝ سَلَامٌ هِيَ حَتَّىٰ مَطْلَعِ الْفَجْرِ ۝}$$

Truly We sent it down
on the Night of Power.
And what will convey to you
what the Night of Power is?
The Night of Power
is better than a thousand months.
In it the angels and the Ruh descend
by their Lord's authority
with every ordinance.

The Presence of the Hour

It is Peace –
until the coming of the dawn.

The words "the angels and the Ruh descend" mean that they come near in the sense mentioned before. They are present. Descend means moving from the high realm, towards that lower realm of normal experience.

On the Laylatul-Qadr we still ourselves with the recitation of Qur'an and dhikr of Allah and by standing and bowing and prostrating, until that which is suspended in presence comes to us and we see it. Then:

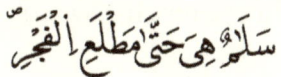

It is Peace – until the coming of the dawn.

In other words, the state does not last forever. We go back into the world, the sun rises and normal life resumes. But we are changed.

We sow the seeds of our intentions for the coming year, and when the blessed 'Eid arrives, the seal of Ramadan is lifted and actions become easy and openings come in the world where before, in the depth of the night, they had come in the non-world.

Many Muslims gather in mosques to look for the Laylatul-Qadr. To the other people outside, coming back from their nights on the town or straggling home from night shifts, it will be as if some people were seen staying in a building at an unreasonable hour, and then leaving in high spirits as the dawn broke. Then the building will stand empty, as before. But what they cannot see is what happened in the hearts: what people took away with them.

The same applies at home. The Muslim rests in preparation for the special night, eats lightly at Iftar, then goes to his or her room and does not reappear until morning. Nothing is seen. But everything important has happened.

The Laylatul-Qadr is a time to put the world behind one's back and direct oneself towards the One.

وَهُوَ بِكُلِّ شَيْءٍ عَلِيمٌ

He has knowledge of all things.

In other words, there is not a thing that can be known, in the past, present or future, which is not already in His knowledge.

They do not measure Allah with His true measure.

Our understanding does not encompass Him but His knowledge encompasses ours. Our job is to raise our expectations of Him and let them soar free. The verb "to be able" only attaches to Allah, subhanahu wa ta'ala, in its unrestricted sense: we only say "Allah can" if we are going to exalt Him above every restraint. But when we say, "I can" or "We can", we make it conditional: "Insha'Allah", because our "can" is only there if He does not remove His "will".

In Ramadan, we invert our days to remind ourselves of this, to let its knowledge permeate us, year upon year, and we pray and go on Hajj, and pay Zakat, to break norms and habits, and to release spontaneity, which opens doors for us. Spontaneity is fostered by guarding the obligations, because the obligations break the chains.

TRUTH AND THE PRAYER

Allah, subhanahu wa ta'ala, says in Surat an-Nur:

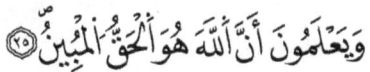

And they will know that Allah is the Clear Truth.

Islam is not a belief system among others or a religion among others. Nor is it, "The belief system that is right, whereas others are wrong." Islam is not a system at all. Nor is it a religion in the sense of a framework or structure which we adopt or enter like a club. That is why the word "convert" is disliked – or even "revert", neither of which has any equivalent in the language of the Qur'an or the language of the Companions. One does not "change religion" by entering Islam. One realises what has been all along.

Islam applies in accordance with the slave's knowledge. What is obligatory is conditional on what we know of the obligations – although there is a minimum of knowledge that it is necessary to acquire.

Iman – belief in Allah – is a gift from Allah even if it comes by the words or actions of another. Once iman is present, there can be action based on it. Action that stems from a believing heart is different. A non-Muslim may abstain from food and drink from dawn to sunset, and may get health benefits, but he cannot attain to the benefits that the Muslim is accustomed to – except by a gift from Allah – because the Muslim restrains his hand based on what he knows and believes. He knows he is seen.

That is why such campaigns as "Fasting for Solidarity" and "Hajj to raise funds for..." are false and infringe upon the rights of Allah, subhanahu wa ta'ala. Allah says in a Hadith Qudsi, "Fasting is mine." Similarly, prostrating in celebration of a football goal is not correct, even though one might feel a certain sympathy for it because it indicates the player's gratitude. And going on Hajj or 'Umrah as a spiritual family holiday is a loss and a descent from greatness.

All belief goes back to Allah, just as all reliance is reliance on Allah. The one who crosses the bridge thinks it will hold him. But Allah ta'ala says:

$$\text{عَلَيْهِ يَتَوَكَّلُ الْمُتَوَكِّلُونَ ۝}$$

All those who truly trust put their trust in Him.

So the kafir trusts the bridge will hold him because, he presumes, it is properly built, but the mumin trusts the bridge will hold him and will do so because it is properly built – because Allah has decreed that the designer was attentive, the builders made no mistakes and the materials were sound. And if it is not, then Allah has decreed that instead. The crack was built in. The difference is between the one who knows he relies on Allah and the one who does not know.

$$\text{هَلْ يَسْتَوِي الَّذِينَ يَعْلَمُونَ وَالَّذِينَ لَا يَعْلَمُونَ}$$

'Are they the same – those who know
and those who do not know?'

Islam is the contract of obedience to the Truth. But we do not 'need Islam'. We need Allah. We are *obliged* to be Muslim.

Allah, may He be exalted, is not in need of Islam or that we conform with it. The Messenger of Allah, may Allah bless him and grant him peace, said that were everyone in the world to do the actions of the best of us, it would not increase Allah, and were everyone in the world to do the actions of the worst of us, it would not take anything away from Allah, subhanahu wa ta'ala.

Islam operates in the realm of understanding and actions, but our understanding and actions do not change, or penetrate, the Truth. The Truth is the way-it-is, beyond qualification. It is not even really the "way things are", since "things" are necessarily experienced in the conditional mode of the senses, which are demonstrably fallible and cannot properly reach the Truth.

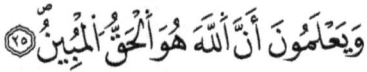

and they will know that Allah is the Clear Truth.

* * *

I would like to mention some of the conditions of the Prayer, because it is advisable to return to the foundations. The things we do in our lives are, as it were, not valid in our balance without the prayer – and Allah knows best – because the first thing we will be asked about when we are questioned on the Last Day will be our prayer.

Prayer is not valid without wudu. Wudu is not valid without intention. We make our intention clear, and our wudu is clear. We wipe our hands, arms, face and feet three times as is preferable. But once is also enough. It is permitted to wipe over leather khuffs, provided wudu was done before donning them, but this does not extend to socks. Socks must be removed, and the *whole* foot must be wiped completely up to above the ankle, including in the gap next to the big toe, but you can leave the other gaps. And the whole of the head must be wiped, from the front hairline to the back hairline.

Ghusl is the whole body, and there is much wisdom in not postponing it after the act of intercourse. The Muslim who is scrupulous and intends to improve himself and his life, stays in ghusl and stays in wudu. If he breaks it, he renews it.

The prayer has its time. Whatever regularly prevents us from praying in time needs to be examined. If it is our work and we cannot reorganise it, then our work has overcome us. If it is the company we regularly keep and we cannot establish the prayer, then that company has overcome us. If it is our laziness and we cannot get hold of ourselves, then we have been defeated by ourselves.

When we take the qibla, we take it according to what we know. A person's prayer is valid even if he points in the opposite direction, provided he thought it was right. And even with correct knowledge, there is a generous margin of error.

In a mosque, we move to the front to pray. It is not good adab to stand at the back of an empty or partly empty mosque and pray alone there. We move forward to the front. The wisdom of this is that it makes us anonymous, because the face is hidden. And it does not force others to walk around us or cross our qibla.

At our homes and at work, men pray together when they can and they seek each other out to do so, with courtesy and consideration. Praying in public is also permissible and can even be advisable, especially in jama'at, provided its provocation or danger does not outweigh its attraction.

In a mosque where there is a regular jama'at, it is, according to the people of Madinah, forbidden and disrespectful to form a second group. If the jama'at in a mosque is finished, we pray separately, however many we may be, because we do not want to cause a split.

The Jumu'a has its own particular rules and courtesies. If we establish a correct Jumu'a, this will benefit us as a jama'at, and as individuals, and it will benefit people around us.

We do not go to Jumu'a as many Christians go to church – just because we are "good Muslims". We go in obedience, with clear knowledge of the immense benefit of attending and because we know the Messenger of Allah went, and the Companions, and all the Muslims, and we know how and when they went. We go with that clarity and intention. So once we have arrived for Jumu'a, we want to do things correctly.

You may do two raka'ats to greet the mosque, but only if the Imam has not yet come in. Once the Imam has come in and taken his place on the Minbar, you may not do anything whatsoever.

The khutba takes the place of the first two raka'ats of Dhuhr. You must do your prayers like your life depends on it, and you must treat the khutba as part of your prayer. The Imam coming in is like the Takbir al-Ihram – after it, you disengage entirely from the world and ignore it.

One sees all sorts of things in mosques. People try to greet each other while the Imam is talking. This is as if you were to arrive at Maghrib, join the prayer line and try to shake hands with the next man.

People arrive and do two raka'ats while the Imam speaks. Not only is this discourteous, it is also invalid. If you arrived at a mosque and found the Jama'at of 'Asr, would you pray two raka'ats before joining it? The sight of someone doing that would disconcert any Muslim who has even the most rudimentary grasp of the Deen. When you come in for Jumu'a and it has already started, sit straight down and listen.

People even look at their phones and messages. What this indicates is that they have completely lost what it means to be performing the prayer. They are in another world.

When the Imam recites out loud, at Jumu'a or in any other prayer, the correct 'ibada, in the Madhhab of the People of Madinah as transmitted by Malik, is to listen. It is not to recite quietly under one's breath, or make du'a, or anything else. It is to listen. Listening *is* the 'ibada. But when he recites silently, we recite silently behind him.

If you put your prayer right, Allah will put you right. Allah, subhanahu wa ta'ala, says in his Noble Book:

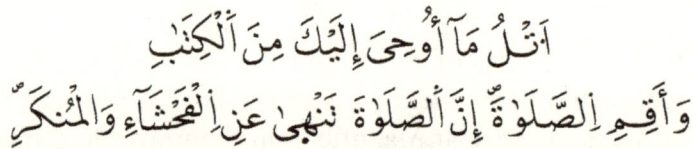

> Recite what has been revealed to you
> of the Book and establish salat.
> Salat precludes indecency and wrongdoing.

The five prayers erect a wall between you and wrong actions. It is very difficult to do anything very bad if you hold to them; and if you hold to them on time, your decree will be transformed to liquid gold in which your mistakes will be forgiven, and Allah knows best.

Were we not to do the five prayers at all, or were we to neglect them, it would be as if we had forgotten the complete and utter power of Allah over us at every moment. It would be as if we had forgotten to thank Allah in the way He has asked, for the mercy and generosity He bestows on us at every moment, even when we cannot see it.

To neglect the five prayers is like entering a comatose state in which all the real good which we might do is put on hold and good actions are in abeyance until we are woken up again, or until our lives are taken from us – and Allah knows best. Yes, we do five prayers because we have been told to. But we do every prayer because we know that Allah has hold of us at every moment, and we feel the debt weighing on us and hope for the vastness of Allah's reward.

We do the prayer so that we have paid the debt, we keep a clean sheet, we keep our house in order, we keep the self in check, we thank Allah five times a day for the million, billion blessings He gives us each day and each second. We mend the ever-decaying boat of good action five times a day, so that we can sail on, by Allah's mercy, and so that when our destiny catches up with us, we are on a voyage of good.

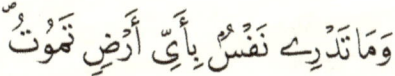

and no self knows in what land it will die.

THE TRANSMISSION OF THE SUNNA

The Hadith are not the same as the Sunna. The Hadith are the *records*, but are not themselves the *behaviour*, which is the Sunna. This is an important distinction, as Hadith are sometimes used indiscriminately to justify all kinds of behaviour.

Somebody once asked me, "If the Hadith are not the Sunna, how is the Sunna transmitted?"

The people of knowledge have divided up the Sunna into four aspects, or, you could say, looked at it from four angles, as it is improper to dismember it.

Firstly, **qawliyya**, or what is spoken. These are the things that the Messenger of Allah, sallallahu 'alayhi wa sallam, said, and they are recorded mainly in Hadith. That is why Hadith necessarily include their narrator or narrators; indeed, the sayings of the Messenger of Allah, sallallahu 'alayhi wa sallam, could only reach paper through other people. There is no line of transmission which is from the Messenger of Allah, to a written Hadith, to the reader. A narrator is always included, since he, sallallahu 'alayhi wa sallam, did not write. The word Hadith means something related.

It is worth staying with this point. He, sallallahu 'alayhi wa sallam, did not write. It was no accident that he was not a man of writing, nor was it a detriment. On the contrary, it was one of his blessings, may Allah bless him and grant him peace, and a gift from Allah to us. This is not a written-down Deen. Allah in his Wisdom brought a Deen which was witnessed and told to others. This is the first part of the answer to the question of how the Sunna is transmitted, and it is important to hold it in mind when we think of and talk about Islam. Namely, that the foremost means by which knowledge and behaviour is transmitted among the human race is by seeing, emulating and absorbing. Writing is a key human activity, but when Allah made the Messenger of Allah a man of example, not writing, He, subhanahu wa ta'ala, was designing our Deen with wisdom and setting up a situation which shows us the primacy of action and speech over the written word.

If we imagine the opposite scenario, that of a Deen being delivered as a book, or a Messenger who wrote down the Deen for people to follow, we can quickly envisage the chaos that would have ensued, since people are wont to interpret written instructions differently, whereas witnessed behaviour and actions are harder to misconstrue.

The Deen was copied by the Companions and absorbed verbally, in actions, adab and states, and this was only written down gradually as the need became clear to them, just as they eventually wrote down and collated the Qur'an.

Second in the categories of Sunna is **fi'liyya**. The things he did, sallallahu 'alayhi wa sallam – and the things the people around him did, and the things the people around them did. This is what is often referred to as the 'Amal. Note, firstly, that it is the actions of the Companions, and even the Followers, as well as the Messenger of Allah, may Allah bless him and grant him peace, that constitute the Sunna. The Sunna is vast, not narrow. The Messenger of Allah, may Allah bless him and grant him peace, said, "My Companions are like stars. You can follow any one of them."

When it is narrated that so-and-so said, "*I saw* the Messenger of Allah *do* such-and-such," then that is a narration of fi'liyya, such as when 'Abdullah ibn 'Umar was seen making his camel turn round in a particular place and was asked why. He said, "I don't know. I once saw the Messenger of Allah doing it, so I do it." So much can be taken from this event, not least the very basis on which we follow him. It is not a rational choice. Nor is it irrational. It is love.

Thirdly, **taqririyya**, the things of which he, sallallahu 'alayhi wa sallam, approved either tacitly or by a gesture or other means of indicating that it was not forbidden, such as when a group of Abyssinians came to the mosque of the Prophet and danced and sang in his praise with their spears, and he called 'Aisha to his side to watch, radiyallahu 'anha, from which we know that such festivities are permitted – but not because he, may Allah bless him and grant him peace, said anything about it. From that can be derived no less the mode in which Muslims everywhere learn their Deen: by accepting what they see around them when it goes on without comment, especially if it is normal practice in their communities. This is a natural and essential part of human behaviour.

Taqririyya truly is a vast affair. You could say: if it is not forbidden, it is permitted. It applies to the great majority of human actions and activities. Taqririyya does not so much give rise to a recorded body of actions, since you cannot record the infinite events which are not commented on; rather it signals an attitude which the healthy Muslim takes: if it is not disallowed, it is allowed.

Furthermore – and this itself is part of the Sunna: it is unbecoming of us to investigate the possibility of something being forbidden if there is nothing to indicate that it might be and nothing calling for its examination. Especially if it is something somebody else is doing. The adab of the Muslim is that we consider the things other people do to be permissible unless there is open evidence to the contrary, and even then it can be better to look away. An example necessitating examination is if the community is at risk from something.

The Muslims are naturally broad-minded: they are of the opinion that things are permitted, provided they are not forbidden. This is based on their confidence in the foundations of existence, and is entirely different from saying that it doesn't matter what is forbidden, or even that all kinds of religions are right, which is not broad-mindedness but the sign of a confused mind and a lack of education. Taqririyya does not apply to things we might do out of ignorance, like mixing other religious festivals with ours, as the Christians did when they combined the celebration of the birth of Jesus with the pagan midwinter festival and placed Easter atop the worship of a fertility goddess in spring. Nor does it mean arbitrary acceptance of all kinds of actions. Rather it shows us that there were many, many things he, may Allah bless him and grant him peace, did not comment on, and that his Companions did not comment on, and which were therefore permitted tacitly or by implication.

Fourthly and finally in the aspects of the Sunna, there is **i'tiqadiyya**, or matters pertaining to belief. This is the deepest aspect of all, because it moves beyond the realm that can be captured in writing, seen physically, or even spoken about. In it are the matters of character which can only be alluded to and described in metaphor or by indication – such as, to give a crude example, "he had the heart of a lion" – and also, matters of manners.

It is said that "manners cannot be taught, only learned" – meaning that the acquisition of adab presupposes a desire to learn. Trying to impose adab upon someone is itself bad manners, with the exception perhaps of bringing up children, and even then there are limitations. The expression "bringing up" means you bring them up – in other words, take them with you upwards, to what hopefully is the higher level of your own behaviour. Other languages make the same allusion, such as 'Erzeihung' in German, which means, literally, pulling. We may only really teach what we ourselves already practice. It is said that a woman came to one of the men of knowledge and asked him to instruct her son to give up the habit of sucking sugar cane. He told her to come back in three days. She returned with her son, and he asked the son to stop, and he did. Afterwards she asked him, "Why did you tell me to come back in three days?" to which he replied, "First I had to give up sugar cane myself."

To return to the Sunna of beliefs, or i'tiqadiyya, it is true that our beliefs can be described in words, otherwise there would be no science of Kalam, but these words point to things that are unseen and the words are therefore signposts, not even labels, let alone identical to the beliefs themselves. The recognition of what these words indicate requires inner certainty, not outer verification.

Thus, as we approach the science of the Sunna of the Inward, or i'tiqadiyya, we depart by degrees from the written record and move further into the blessed realm of face-to-face transmission.

The Transmission of the Sunna

The Messenger of Allah, sallallahu 'alayhi wa sallam, said, "If you stay with someone for forty days, you become like them." That is because our beliefs, manners, bearing and interactions are learned not from books, but from spending time with others and taking on their ways.

While this process of transmission escapes outward verification and record, it is at the same time the most trustworthy channel by which the Sunna, and indeed any action, can be handed down. It is at the very heart of the Sunna. While we may argue about Hadith and their applicability, and debate fiqh judgments, logic and the interpretation of words, once we enter the realm of hearts, we enter the zone of unanimous agreement. While the Fuqaha debate, there is no disagreement among the people of certainty.

* * *

The Sunna is the whole process by which the Companions saw, witnessed and took on the ways of our Messenger, may Allah bless him and grant him peace, and how they themselves acted upon this and lived their lives.

And that is how it is transmitted to us.

What we know of our Deen, we learn from those around us. It is true that we may reinforce and augment this by reading books, including the Hadith, and they may greatly illuminate our knowledge. But reading is not essential to being a Muslim or even to being a knowledgeable Muslim. Indeed, reading about the Deen ought to be brought into balance by our interactions with our Muslim brothers and sisters and the society at large.

I will give you an example. It is Sunna to eat with the right hand. It would be odd to imagine that we all learned that by reading it in a Hadith. Our parents probably told us, and if not, then our companions told us, or we noticed it in gatherings and asked, and it was discussed and affirmed. This very process is itself one of the adornments of Islam – the visual and verbal transmission of the Sunna by people who love it and wish others to know about it.

But the Sunna is also *how* we tell others. I know a man who used to sport a rather long moustache which hung a little way over his top lip. Because he is a man of sensitivity, he would not allow any old person to tell him what was right or wrong, on top of which he has the natural dignity of someone aware of their own appearance. One day, he told me, "I used to wear a long moustache that went a little beyond the lip, and one of the brothers told me it was the Sunna for the moustache not to go down over the lip. Ever since then, I have trimmed it. But if it hadn't been that person who told me, whom I trust, and if he hadn't told me in a good way, I never would have done it."

Shaykh 'Abdalqadir as-Sufi related something similar

to me. He said that when he had recently become Muslim, he had long fingernails, and one of the wise men pointed to them and made a gesture of cutting. He said that at first he felt offended. But then the old man said, emphatically and with love, "Sunna!" and the Shaykh realised it was not about the man's personal opinion or taste. He wanted something good for him. This courtesy stems from the inner condition of the transmitter and the readiness of the recipient – and those are themselves Sunna. We cannot separate the technicalities of the Sunna from the Sunna of transmission and courtesy. The one lives only through the other.

At the very heart of this matter is Certainty, which is the very source of 'aqida.

Allah refers to this in His Noble Book:

$$\text{إِنَّ هَٰذَا لَهُوَ حَقُّ ٱلْيَقِينِ ۝ فَسَبِّحْ بِٱسْمِ رَبِّكَ ٱلْعَظِيمِ ۝}$$

This is indeed the Truth of Certainty.
So glorify the Name of your Lord, the Magnificent!

Certainty is seen by the one who has seen it, known by the one who has tasted it, and possessed by the one possessed by it. Certainty *is* Sunna. Can you write it down? No. You witness someone with certainty, and you want it yourself.

I said at the beginning that Hadith are used indiscriminately to justify all kinds of behaviour. It is unsurprising that this is so, since the dominant social ethos gives primacy to information as knowledge and no longer understands the importance of manners, keeping company, or inner certainty.

But despite the predominance of information-knowledge, Allah has protected the Sunna of His Messenger by sustaining its transmission along proper pathways. The Sunna, and indeed the whole of Islam, has been transmitted to us as it was to the Companions, by close association with people who know and by copying them, asking them, witnessing what is commonly accepted and established and conforming to the practices of our communities. The long passage of time is not able to inhibit this process if Allah wishes to preserve it – especially when it comes to inner matters or i'tiqadiyya, the Sunna of beliefs, inner states and certainty, which can be acquired by seeking out and spending time with people who have become the receptacles of some of the inner states and knowledges of the Messenger of Allah, sallallahu 'alayhi wa sallam.

I wish to express my gratitude to those who have transmitted the Sunna to us, and also the asker of the question, how is the Sunna transmitted. His asking was a strong Sunna, and he is one of the illuminators of our community.

LEADERSHIP, WORK, HELPING PEOPLE

Allah, subhanahu wa ta'ala, says in His mighty Book:

$$\text{الَّذِينَ يَذْكُرُونَ اللَّهَ قِيَامًا وَقُعُودًا وَعَلَىٰ جُنُوبِهِمْ وَيَتَفَكَّرُونَ فِي خَلْقِ السَّمَاوَاتِ وَالْأَرْضِ رَبَّنَا مَا خَلَقْتَ هَٰذَا بَاطِلًا سُبْحَانَكَ فَقِنَا عَذَابَ النَّارِ}$$

Those who remember Allah,
standing, sitting and lying on their sides,
and reflect on the creation
of the heavens and the earth:
'Our Lord, You have not created this for nothing.
Glory be to You!
So safeguard us from the punishment of the Fire.'

Look at and reflect on the birds and animals. Every type of leadership is evident among them, from the subtle to the obvious, and all of their possibilities are contained within us. Have you seen flocks of starlings murmurating in great swarms, like fluids respondent? Scientists have discovered that each movement originates with one bird, and that bird's movement is transmitted to the nearest seven. Each of those birds then passes the movement on to the next seven. The effect is almost instantaneous, however large the flock. The flock does not actually move in unison in the technical sense; it follows the leading bird so gracefully and quickly that a smooth motion is produced. The same happens in shoals of fish.

We humans, in the Prophetically revealed pattern which is natural to us, need leadership to function.

Any Muslim who lives in a community but has not acknowledged a leader of that community is sooner or later living unnaturally. The Messenger of Allah, sallallahu 'alayhi wa sallam, said that he who dies without giving allegiance to an Amir dies the death of jahiliyya.

Every one of us is engaged in some kind of political or social activity, whether actively or passively. To claim that we stay out of politics, and to actively refuse to choose a political position, merely means that we assign ourselves to the great passive mass, manipulated in whatever way the current age prefers.

I am not talking about party politics, campaigning, or marching. I am talking about politics in the broadest sense, in the way we collectively influence each other, decide on our activities and engage in the society we are in. As soon as we accept leadership in a Muslim community, we actively engage in the world in a way which has nothing to do with party-politics – in fact it is a different species of politics altogether. And it has a profound impact on the wellbeing of ourselves, our families and the people in our community. It also affects the wider society, because they will see us differently under positive leadership.

And yet leadership in community is not a matter of one man deciding everything and everyone else following. Like the starlings in the flock, every member is inescapably affected by the others. No man governs alone.

The leader himself has a heavy responsibility, and in this age, when personal political leadership is frowned upon, one of the leader's most urgent responsibilities is to present activities that inspire other people to join him and lend a hand. Our unity emerges in action.

However: the leader, and the circle around him who wish to advise and assist most closely, must be free, and not bondsmen – not tied in obedience to others.

It is well to reflect on the nature of your working situation, because it can impact on your freedom and your ability to help.

People in our era seek employment, and understandably so. A society's success is sometimes measured by the percentage of adults in employment. In this country, if you are not employed, you are likely to end up on social welfare, thus dependent on the state.

Employment, although to most people preferable to welfare payments, is itself only a tiny step towards actual independence. In fact, it is still dependency.

The employment contract typically requires that you give over eight hours of your day, five days a week, to your employer. You are left with the evenings and weekends, plus a few weeks a year for a change of scene to release the tensions accumulated in your bonded situation.

The fixed-hours week is designed to take precisely those hours which you can realistically dedicate to productivity and creativity, and hand them to your employer. You are paid to put yourself at their disposal for that time; which is, from a productive point of view, all of your time. What you are left with is a series of recovery phases.

This situation does not befit our leaders, or anybody else who wishes to be actively engaged in serving society, because it stops them putting anything above their jobs, except perhaps their families.

I am not advocating the end of employment or the abandonment of salaried jobs. I am encouraging you to think about the choices you make.

If you wish to help your leader, then you need not dedicate your entire day to him. But there will be times when you need to put him first.

If you wish to help the Muslims, you need not hand over your entire life to them. But there will be times when you need to put them first.

If you wish to effect positive change in society, you need not spend all your working hours in the service of higher aims. But there will be times when you need to put others first.

You need to be in a position to put important things first.

To do that, you need to be in charge of your own time, so that when circumstances call for action, you can act.

Again, I am not advocating the abandonment of jobs or work. For many people at many times, salaried employment may be the best strategy. I am encouraging you to examine those intentions and choices that will affect your future and affect the health and success of our Muslim community.

Every community needs a core group who are free to act and free to prioritise the affairs of others. They may still work for their living and provide for their families, and indeed will be successful in doing so. But serving the wellbeing of others is the highest calling.

The key to escaping what can be the trap of salaried employment is to combine with others and break free together. Sit down with them face to face, mention Allah's Name, and work out what to do. You will succeed.

Everything is formed on its intention. Rasul, sallallahu 'alayhi wa sallam, said, "Innama-l-'Amaalu bi-n-Niyyat," – actions are by intentions.

If you intend good with Allah, you will have good.

If you intend good for the slaves of Allah, they will have good and you will have good and a reward.

If you act with the intention of freeing yourself so that you can prioritise higher work, then you will get what you ask for, and you will not lose money or security. Security – 'al-Aman' – is with Allah. Al-Aman is the sense of feeling safe. How many people who thought they were secure, came undone? And how many people who relied on Allah in tenuous situations were carried from safety to safety by miracles?

I wish to remind you of your own love and your own mighty power, which is Allah's power. You are the Askers of Allah, you are the Givers in the Name of Allah, the Visitors in the Way of Allah, who can bring your gifts to anyone you please. All of mankind lies in its sickbed waiting for you, because they do not know what you know. You are the nurses, and they are the patients. They do not know the simple things that are common knowledge to us, like knowing that we will go to Allah with our balance. Like the fact that the Messenger of Allah said we must wash the dead body and bury it straight away. Like knowing that if we invite people to eat with us for Allah, we and they will benefit. These are the messages we must tell people.

The people are sick. Visit them. You need not visit them all – one or two will suffice. Think again of the murmurating starlings – each of us affects the nearest six or seven and that is sufficient to change the direction of millions. Visit your neighbours. If they like to talk of God, talk to them. If not, your presence will still change them.

Spread small kindnesses and abandon bad opinion. You will bring life and healing to people you do not even know.

And ask Allah for them. The du'a is the weapon of the mumin.

One of the Awliya of our community said to me, "With medicine, if you believe that the healing lies in it, then that will be the medicine which heals you." This was like a commentary on Allah's words in a Hadith Qudsi, "I am in my slave's opinion of Me," or, translated differently, "I will be to you what you think I will be."

The commentators have said about this Hadith Qudsi, that the slave will be forgiven if he asks, his hardship will be relieved if he asks, his tawba will be accepted if he repents, and so on. We say, this commentary only tells part of the story. If we ask Allah to help other people, He will help them. If we ask Allah to bring Islam to the people, however far from it they may seem to be, He will do so. We are permitted to elevate our expectations to heights verging on the impossible, and then to raise them further still. That is closer to Tawhid than having realistic expectations. The Messenger of Allah, peace and blessings of Allah be upon him, said, "When you ask Allah, ask strongly, do not say 'do such-and-such if You will,' because there is no compelling Allah."

We ask Allah to make us ask for what is the very highest we can ask for, and then to ask for even more.

THE EMERGENCE OF MEANING

Allah, subhanahu wa ta'ala, says in Qur'an:

وَمَا خَلَقْتُ الْجِنَّ وَالْإِنسَ إِلَّا لِيَعْبُدُونِ ۝

I only created jinn and man to worship Me.

Not only has He, may He be exalted, ordered us to worship Him. He tells us unequivocally that He did not create us for anything else. Humans without worship are like food that is not eaten. They are wasted.

I am not suggesting that we should have no aims and live humble lives without material aspiration, praying and doing little else. But we can begin to realise that going beyond the perpetual pursuit of material aims has something to do with worship. When the believer seriously takes on worship – 'ibada – either he starts to do the acts of worship which before he was aware of but did not do, or he begins to inhabit and actively imbue with meaning and awareness the rites which before he did, but only out of hollow obedience, devoid of any real expectation.

When we take on worship, the journey has in one sense only just begun. We have donned the clothes of Islam, but that in itself does not assuage the old, familiar drives for material things. But: it does change our understanding of them. Somehow we know something is now different. Rescued in the ship of the Five Prayers, the Ship of Fasting, the Ship of Shahada, the Ship of Hajj and the Ship of Zakat, we come to see that we had been sinking, drowning in a sea of pointlessness, going darkly down to a dismal destination, and that we were plucked out by a change of destiny which was neither of our making nor by the doing of others, even if their and our words and actions were instrumental in what happened.

A voyage in the ship of meaning, atop the dark and surging seas of ignorance, has begun, but we may not entirely know the destination. Nevertheless, the journey can begin.

Allah ta'ala says:

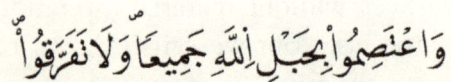

The Emergence of Meaning

> Hold fast to the rope of Allah all together,
> and do not separate.

Let us look at two aspects of this.

"Hold tight to the rope of Allah," and "All together, do not separate."

The rope which we have to grasp hold of is the Deen. It is the obligatory acts of worship. The words, "Do not separate" and "All together" mean we perform these acts with each other and we are on this Deen with each other.

Shaykh Muhammad ibn al-Habib, says in his Diwan:

$$\text{وَارْكَبْ سَفِينَةَ سُنَّةٍ تَنْجُو بِهَا}$$
$$\text{وَاسْلُكْ سَبِيلَ رَئِيسِهَا فِي هَوَاهُ}$$

> Board the ship of the Sunna
> and you will be rescued in it,
> and travel the path of its captain in his love.

The ship of the Sunna is how we find out how to understand the things that drive us.

But the transforming element is in Allah's words, "All together" and "Do not separate." This means clinging on to each other, seeking company and avoiding being alone.

Ibn 'Umar narrated that the Messenger of Allah, sallallahu 'alayhi wa sallam, said, "If people were to know what I know about being alone, no one would ever travel by night alone." It is said that the wolf devours the sheep that finds itself away from the flock. It is also said that coals left in the hearth keep glowing. But remove a glowing coal and place it on its own, and it turns dark.

I do not wish to be rigid and frighten anybody about times they might find themselves alone, especially in this strange society we live in where aloneness is so endemic, there is now a Minister of Loneliness. But we must make it our habit to seek good company.

Once in the company of other wayfarers, the journey is transformed. The joys and the sorrows, experienced, discussed and reflected on with other similarly inclined travellers, begin to take on a transformative meaning previously veiled from us.

Allah ta'ala says:

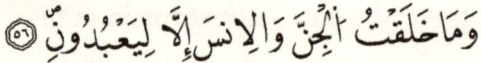

I only created jinn and man to worship Me.

After the heartache and disappointment of obtaining or not obtaining material things, the wayfarer realises, "I was looking in the wrong direction all the time. I need to try to travel towards my Lord, so that I do the

The Emergence of Meaning

worship for which I was created. I must stop facing material needs."

It is also when the wayfarer realises that it is not just the five prayers that are meant by the word 'worship', but that the whole of life can be transformed into that worship which he seeks somehow to wholly embrace. I do not mean Islamicising everything and imagining we can avoid the dirt of the world. But the word 'ibada is from 'abd, slave, and when we do things *knowing* we are slaves of Allah, our actions are worshipful.

The Messenger of Allah, sallallahu 'alayhi wa sallam, was like that all the time, without interruption. So the wayfarer wants to know him.

Again:

وَارْكَبْ سَفِينَةَ سُنَّةٍ تَنْجُو بِهَا
وَاسْلُكْ سَبِيلَ رَئِيسِهَا فِي هَوَاهُ

> Board the ship of the Sunna
> and you will be rescued in it,
> and travel the path of its captain in his love.

So the wayfarer wants to know the Messenger of Allah, and he discovers the rescue that lies in his Sunna, sallallahu 'alayhi wa sallam.

The Sunna is not about long beards or covering up bits of women's bodies.

It is about the tremendous, urgent inner question: "What did he, sallallahu 'alayhi wa sallam, do in this situation? What was he like? What was his inner experience? How did he respond to the things that people came to him with – and how should I respond to what I am faced with? How can I do things the way he did? How can I become more like him, sallallahu 'alayhi wa sallam? How can I stay in his company all the time so I am never left without a way forward?" In fact, how awful is it to live for a moment absent from him?

We cannot attain his level. But from this quest to follow him, Allah ta'ala begins to give us little portions. Little gifts. Little fragments of his behaviour that take residence in the character of the wayfarer. These are the gifts of the Sunna, and he begins to want more, to be hungry. And he begins to hide these gifts beneath a mantle of normality.

What is the main channel through which the wayfarer obtains these gifts of the Sunna? It is through spending time with other slaves of Allah to whom Allah has already granted some of these knowledges and noble behaviour.

We see someone who has a particular Sunna, and we are jealous of it with a permitted jealousy. We say to ourselves, "I want what he or she has. I want Allah to give it to me too." And it begins to happen.

Then the wayfarer is told by the Messenger of Allah, sallallahu 'alayhi wa sallam, "Anyone who blesses me ten times, will be blessed a hundred times. Anyone who blesses me a hundred times, will be blessed a thousand times. And anyone who blesses me a thousand times will be freed from the Fire."

So he takes on the prayer on the Prophet. What we sing after the Prayer, "Allahumma salli 'ala sayyidina Muhammad...." is taking us on that journey. Five prayers, and we have prayed for Allah's blessings for him fifteen times and got hundreds of blessings. Five days, we have asked blessings on him forty-five times. Five weeks and we are already half way to a thousand blessings on him.

Then there are his words, sallallahu 'alayhi wa sallam, narrated by Abu Umama, when he said, "Do ghusl on the day of Jumu'a, because whoever does ghusl on Jumu'a will have all the wrong actions he committed from one Jumu'a to the next forgiven as well as three additional days."

In other words: you need only do the normal things we do as practising Muslims, and you are promised so much forgiveness that it would be inconceivable not to be forgiven.

At this point it dawns on the wayfarer, that from drowning in a sea of meaninglessness, he has not only been rescued, he is now being drowned in a sea of mercy, light and forgiveness, from which he cannot escape.

The journey of the wayfarer is turned on its head.

The struggles are not gone, the joys and sorrows are still there, the fears and hopes are still there, the expansions and contractions are still there. But they are experienced differently. And from being concerned with his urges, he is now becoming concerned that it is Allah who knows the contents of his heart, so he hands his concerns over to Allah, subhanahu wa taʻala.

Surat al-Anʻam 60:

$$\text{وَمَا تَسْقُطُ مِن وَرَقَةٍ إِلَّا يَعْلَمُهَا}$$

No leaf falls without Allah's knowing it.

All of the things that happen to him are from Allah. The struggle now is not, "How do I get away from these unpleasant things and run to happiness?" The wayfarer begins to examine the things he once ran away from. Allah, subhanahu wa taʻala, says in Surat al-Baqara:

$$\text{وَعَسَىٰ أَن تَكْرَهُوا۟ شَيْـًٔا وَهُوَ خَيْرٌ لَّكُمْ}$$

It may be that you hate something
when it is good for you.

But Allah also says, in Surat al-Fatir:

$$\text{مَّا يَفْتَحِ ٱللَّهُ لِلنَّاسِ مِن رَّحْمَةٍ فَلَا مُمْسِكَ لَهَا}$$
$$\text{وَمَا يُمْسِكْ فَلَا مُرْسِلَ لَهُۥ مِنۢ بَعْدِهِۦ وَهُوَ ٱلْعَزِيزُ ٱلْحَكِيمُ ۝}$$

The Emergence of Meaning

Any mercy Allah opens up to people,
no-one can withhold,
and any mercy He withholds,
no-one can afterwards release.
He is the Almighty, the All-Wise.

FUTURE UNCERTAINTY

Surat Ibrahim:

$$\text{وَءَاتَىٰكُم مِّن كُلِّ مَا سَأَلْتُمُوهُ وَإِن تَعُدُّوا۟ نِعْمَتَ ٱللَّهِ لَا تُحْصُوهَآ}$$

He has given you everything you have asked Him for. If you tried to number Allah's blessings, you could never count them.

As I was writing this down in the final days of Ramadan, I realised that this blessed Jumu'a could be the 30th day of Ramadan or it could be the blessed 'Eid. Such future uncertainty is one of the mighty secrets of Islam and one of its gifts.

We do not know what any day holds, but it can often seem as if we know what lies ahead. The world and its routines can veil the real situation, which is that every single thing in front of us is unknown. But Allah has set up time in days, varying the night and day with extraordinary regularity. He, glory be to Him, says many times in Qur'an:

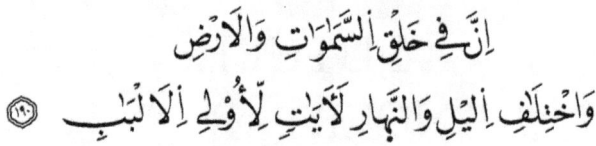

In the creation of the heavens and the earth,
and the alternation of night and day,
there are Signs for people with intelligence.

This pattern gives us a semblance of regularity and predictability, yet despite this, none of us really knows where we will be tomorrow, let alone next year. Allah, the Vast, says in Qur'an, in Surat Luqman:

وَمَا تَدْرِي نَفْسٌ بِأَيِّ أَرْضٍ تَمُوتُ

and no self knows in what land it will die.

Muslims are able to maintain a healthy outlook because of our Deen's many reminders of life's uncertainty. For example: it is our practice to say, "I will do such-and-such, Insha'Allah." While this word may sometimes be used too lightly, properly speaking we say it not about any old event in the future, or about the actions of others, but in conjunction with our own statements of intent, as in the ayat, in Surat al-Kahf:

$$\text{وَلَا تَقُولَنَّ لِشَاْىْءٍ اِنِّى فَاعِلٌ ذَالِكَ غَدًا ۝ اِلَّا أَنْ يَشَاءَ اللَّهُ}$$

> Never say about anything,
> 'I am doing that tomorrow,'
> without adding 'If Allah wills.'

So we say, "I will come and see you tomorrow, Insha'Allah" – if Allah wills – to remind ourselves that we will only fulfil our intention if Allah wants us to. It is not really correct to say, "Insha'Allah it will be good weather tomorrow" when what we really mean to say is, *we hope* it will be good weather. Of course, this will only happen if Allah wills, but we have no part in it, so there is no need to disguise our hopes in a statement of 'aqida – except if we wish to *ask* Allah for good weather, which would be more appropriate. But Allah knows best what people mean. Perhaps people say 'Insha'Allah' and mean it as a du'a, in which case, may they be rewarded.

As well as future uncertainty, there are also uncertainties inherent in judgments of fiqh. It is a tendency of man to try to eliminate uncertainty from life, and the fiqh has not been spared this. But properly speaking, all legal decisions are objectively uncertain.

I will give you an example. When you fall asleep in wudu then wake up, are you in wudu? The answer is that if somebody would have called your name and you would have awoken, you are still in wudu, but if you were sleeping so deeply you would have slept on, you are no longer in wudu. Can that be quantified or examined by somebody else? Of course not. It is entirely dependent on an assessment process inside you, and furthermore it is an estimate, since in all likelihood, nobody actually came and said your name. This matter becomes weightier for someone who leads the prayer. He must say to himself: will the prayer be valid, not only for me but for everyone else? It is impossible to make proper judgments without fear of Allah.

In fact, it is impossible to have any law without taqwa, since it must be admitted that however strong the evidence of an event, it is only ever perceived through the senses and memory, which are demonstrably fallible. Since the kuffar deny the afterlife in which the matter of justice will be finally settled, it is unsurprising that they are unwilling to accept the death penalty, even for crimes which manifestly warrant it, because there is always the risk of wrong judgment, and they live in the pretence that death is the absolute end, even though they know otherwise.

The same inherent uncertainty applies to civic judgments, such as the day of 'Eid. The 'Eid is defined as the day after the new moon at the end of Ramadan has been sighted by the naked eye by at least two sound witnesses. If only one person saw it, it is not 'Eid – although that one man breaks his fast in secret. 'Eid, therefore, is not an objective fact, it only exists by virtue of the witnesses, the conditions, and the leader who announces it, and by the fact that we have obeyed Allah and fasted the month leading up to it, without which it would be meaningless.

Over time, and with a weakening of people's understanding of the fiqh, the 'Eid has in many places become a calendar event, stated in advance. This is incorrect, because until the moon is actually sighted, or until 30 days have been fasted, there can be no 'Eid. Why has this happened the world over?

It is perhaps understandable that many Muslims have felt the need to conform, faced with a dominant structuralist world in which the elimination of future uncertainty has become an unquestioned ideal.

The stronger position, however, is to allow the rest of the world to rush towards structuralism while we hold to the natural pattern shown to us by the Messenger of Allah – the Messenger of the One in Whose Hand the future lies.

I will give you another example. Here in this community, the leadership has the wisdom and confidence to allow the 'Eid and its prayer, and the cessation of fasting, to fall on its proper day, according to the sighting of the moon by competent authorities. In our small community this is easy, but in a large Muslim society, it might seem to have more complicated implications. The society's planners may ask, looking ahead to this day, "Do we make it a public holiday, and if so, what happens if it turns out to be a day of fasting?"

Economists might argue that an unnecessary public holiday damages the economy. And do the managers of large institutions like government offices and food management companies that supply tens of thousands of people plan regular meals for that uncertain day, or do they plan an early breakfast and iftar? Again, their economists might object to the potential waste involved in such uncertainty.

And, do the stock exchanges in the Muslim capitals say to their partners in London and New York, "We do not know what day our festival falls on, so we take both days off while you trade on and make your billions without us?"

Whatever the reasons, most Muslim governments have taken the step of fixing the date of 'Eid years in advance, using astrological calculations. Not only that, but they seem to use the theoretical date on which the moon is born, rather than the date on which it could be seen, so that year after year we have countries declaring 'Eid on evenings and in places where no human being could possibly see the moon with the naked eye, and Muslims in other countries following them.

It would be worthwhile for Muslim academics to study the origins of this deviation, and to identify the people involved in it, just as it is worthwhile studying the origins of so-called Islamic stock exchanges and the people involved in them, so that we can understand the mistakes, weaknesses, lack of imagination and lack of 'aqida that has led us to such an unnatural situation.

I say lack of 'aqida because every deviation in the fiqh originates in a weakness of 'aqida. What we believe about Allah affects everything we do and every decision we make.

We must be scrupulous in what we say about Allah, and we need to find in ourselves the ability to articulate our Deen to the wider world in a way that befits it. This is the way given to us by the One Who governs all of man's affairs and by Whose permission everything either succeeds or fails. Allah's words:

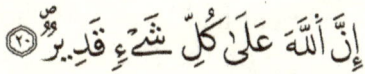

Allah has power over all things –

– are repeated many times in His mighty Book. There have been groups of Muslims through the ages who have so deeply recognised the importance of ayats describing Allah's absolute power, that they have undertaken to recite them many times a day, and have become imbued with an awareness which carries them from one success to another.

When we understand Allah's absolute power over all things and all events, then we become able to explain to other people that the way His Messenger shows us is best, and that if it seems at variance with what is taken to be customary, then it is the custom which needs to be reassessed.

So the message from the Muslims to the stock exchanges of New York and London, if indeed we even decide to talk to them, is that we do not know the exact date of our festival, just as they do not know the exact date of their crash.

On the subject of stock exchanges, we could add that while mankind suffers in different ways throughout the world in different ages, here and now, the oppression we are under is financial.

On 5 June 2018, it was quietly reported in the news that the British government had lost two billion pounds on the sale of just 7.7% of the shares in the Royal Bank of Scotland, which it bailed out (a euphemism for gifting money to) after the financial crisis of 2008. The government had given so much money to this privately owned bank to rescue it, that selling just 7.7% of shares in it at half the buying price incurred a loss of two thousand, thousand, thousand pounds.

Two thousand, thousand, thousand pounds – a mere blip on the screen of criminal finance that carries on in this and every other country. No wonder the man on the street feels a sense of financial constriction, but cannot really say why. He is working to pay for these actions.

I will give you another example. The money it takes to put someone through university used to be provided from tax revenues. Now, at the insinuation of banks and economists, students have been made to borrow this money, so that people entering university today will have average debts of fifty thousand pounds by the time they graduate. The economists may say, what does it matter whether it comes out of the tax of their parents or their own subsequent earnings?

They may well say that, because they and their institutions are creating a slave population inured to debt repayment. It could be argued that student debts are government loans at low interest. But student loans force newly emerging adults to capitulate completely to massive institutional endebtment, a pattern they will then go on following for life, mostly without question. They become the foodstuff of financiers.

It is the crime of the practice of usury which permits this situation to go on, and which we must confront, but not with violence or protest for the sake of protest, which will bring defeat. To see the effective strategy for doing so, we live in active expectation of the moment to act, like the cat at the mouse-hole. Just as we live in great expectation of personal illumination, we live in anticipation of social renewal, at our hands or those of our children. May Allah make them and us victorious in His Way.

What is the correct 'aqida which will set us on firm foundations when we act? One of the great 'Ulama to formulate the 'aqida was Qadi 'Iyad, may Allah be pleased with him, in his Qawa'id al-Islam. He says that the ten things we necessarily accept are:

1. That Allah is One, undivided in His Essence.
2. That there is no second with Him in His divinity.
3. That He is Living, Self-Subsistent.
4. That He is neither diminished by time nor does sleep overtake Him.
5. That He is the God of everything and its Creator.
6. That He has power over everything.
7. That He knows what is outwardly apparent and what is inwardly hidden.
8. That He wills every created thing – bad or good.
9. That He hears, sees and speaks without any bodily parts and without instrument – rather, His hearing, seeing and speech are some of His attributes, and His attributes do not resemble ordinary attributes – they are not like ours.
10. Similarly, His Essence does not resemble ordinary essences.

Qadi 'Iyad continues:

1. We accept that coming into being in time is impossible for Him, may He be exalted.
2. That non-existence is impossible for Him – rather, He is by His attributes and names Pre-Existent, Going-On, Eternally Existent, standing in judgment over every self for what it has earned. He has no first and no last – rather, *'He is the First and the Last.'*
3. That it is impossible that there is a god other than Him.
4. That it is impossible that He is not independent of all His creation, and impossible that He needs any supporter in His kingship.

5. That it is impossible that one affair takes His attention from another in His decreeing and His giving orders.
6. That it is impossible that any place in His heavens or His earth contains Him – rather He is as He was before the creation of place.
7. That it is impossible that He is either substance or body or that He has a shape or a form, or that anything resembles Him and that He has a likeness – rather He is the One, the Eternally Self-Subsistent Who has not given birth, nor was He born, nor does He have any equal.
8. That it is impossible that events and changes change Him or that defects and damage reach Him.
9. That it is impossible that injustice attaches to Him – rather the whole of His decree is wisdom and justice.
10. That it is impossible that any of the acts of His creation is without His decree and His act of creation and His will.

We also accept:

1. That Allah, may He be exalted, sent His Prophets and His Messengers to His slaves.
2. That He sent down on them His signs and His books.
3. That he sealed messengerhood with our Prophet Muhammad, may Allah bless him and grant him peace.
4. That He *'sent down on him the Qur'an as a guidance for mankind with clear proofs in its guidance and discrimination.'*
5. That it is the speech of our Lord, neither created nor creating.
6. That the Prophet, may Allah bless him and grant him peace, was truthful in what he told.

7. That his law abrogates all the other laws.
8. That the Garden and the Fire are real.
9. That they are both in existence, prepared for the people of misery and the people of happiness.
10. That the angels are real – some of them recording, writing the deeds of the slaves, and some of them messengers of Allah to His Prophets, and some of them *'severe, harsh angels who do not disobey Allah in what He orders them to do and who do as they are commanded.'*

1. We accept that this world will come to an end and *'everything that is on it will come to an end.'*
2. That people will be tried in their graves and they will be given ease or given torment therein.
3. That Allah will gather them together on the Day of Rising – as He made them originally, so they will return.
4. That the Reckoning and the Balance are real.
5. That the Path (Sirat) over the Fire to the Garden is real.
6. That the Pond (Hawd) is real.
7. That the people of right action will be in bliss in the Garden.
8. That the kafirun will be in the Fire in intense heat.
9. That the muminun will see Allah, the Mighty, the Majestic, with their eyesight in the Next World.

We ask Allah, the Great and Majestic, to give us clarity and certainty and correctness in everything we believe, and to steer us away from incorrect beliefs that will lead us to wrong actions.

We ask Allah, subhanahu wa ta'ala, to bless and protect our leadership and everyone who serves and helps the Muslims.

We ask Allah, subhanahu wa ta'ala, to prepare us for great actions, by Him and for Him, seeking forgiveness from Him and in great expectation of His victory.

JUSTICE OF THE DECREE AND FREE WILL

Allah ta'ala says in His Noble Book:

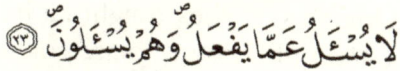

He will not be questioned about what He does,
but they will be questioned.

Recently a young person asked me why, if Allah has power over everything, do some people get punished and sent to the Fire? The implication was that there is an element of injustice or cruelty. While this might be considered an impertinent question because it oversteps the proper adab with our Lord, may He be exalted, we can give it some latitude on account of the youth of the asker and the environment we find ourselves in, which could be described as a Christian society, or, more properly, a post-Christian society.

Given this post-Christian context, and because the question may have been aggravated by that context, it is worthwhile mentioning the mistake of the Christians, since their seminal deviation gave rise to the character and colouring of their psychology, which shapes the environment in which many of us grew up and in which many of our children are immersed.

Allah, may He be exalted, says in the Fatiha:

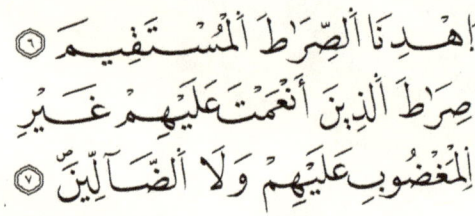

Guide us on the Straight Path,
The Path of those who are guided,
Not of those with anger on them,
Or the misguided.

The latter group whom we seek not to follow, those who are misguided, are the Christians. What is the misguidance of the Christians? It is that they elevated their Prophet, Sayyiduna 'Issa, 'alayhi salam, to the station of divinity by calling him the son of God.

Allah ta'ala says in His Noble Book:

> Allah is only One God.
> He is too Glorious to have a son!
> Everything in the heavens and in the earth
> belongs to Him.
> Allah suffices as a Guardian.

What is revealed in these ayats is that, if it were as they claim, that God had a son, it would throw doubt on His perfect elevation above any human standards. To illustrate this point, one might say, in deduction from the ayats: if God were to have had a son, then He would not have sufficed as a guardian. By saying that Jesus was the son of God, they are diminishing Allah, may He be exalted above what they say, and may Allah protect us from holding such beliefs. This mistake of theirs is the origin of the aberration in their psychology and it opens the door to misunderstanding the Decree.

The Christians are noted for posing this question of why God should cause so much suffering in the world. Again, it is not a correct question, but we are allowing ourselves to pay attention to it, since the intention is to keep our own understanding clear.

By ascribing human states such as fatherhood to Allah – may Allah protect us! – the Christians veil themselves from recognising the full perfection of Allah's true Attributes. By ascribing human functions to their Lord, such as parenthood, they allow themselves to measure their Lord by the standards of mankind.

Allah ta'ala says in His Book:

وَمَا قَدَرُوا ٱللَّهَ حَقَّ قَدْرِهِۦ

They do not measure Allah with His true measure.

His Attributes are not like our attributes and His Essence does not resemble our essence. That is why we avoid uttering words that might trespass upon any suggestion of semblance, partnership or likening.

Qadi 'Iyad says, "It is not permitted to use the conjunction 'and' (*wa*) in connection with Allah in the case of anyone except the Prophet. Hudhayfa said that the Prophet said, "None of you should say, 'What Allah wills and so-and-so wills.' Rather say, 'What Allah wills.' Then stop and say, 'So-and-so wills.'" Al-Khattabi said, "The Prophet has guided you to correct behaviour in putting the will of Allah before the will of others. He chose 'then' (*thumma*) which implies sequence and deference as opposed to 'and' (*wa*) which implies partnership."

Something similar is mentioned in another Hadith. Someone was speaking in the presence of the Prophet, may Allah bless him and grant him peace, and said, "Whoever obeys Allah and His Messenger has been rightly guided, and whoever rebels against them both (joining them together by using the dual form)..." The Prophet stopped him and said, "What a bad speaker you are! Get up!" He, may Allah bless him and grant him peace, did not want to hear anything articulated that way.

Justice of the Decree and Free Will

Allah sent down Surat al-Ikhlas and made it short and easy to memorise. After the Fatiha, it is the most-recited Surat in the Qur'an.

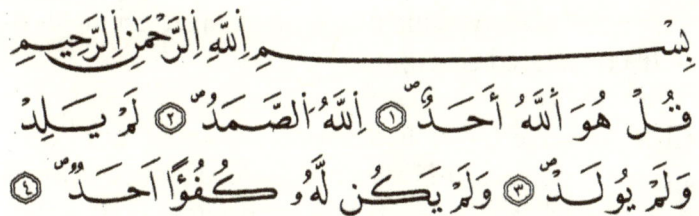

Say: 'He is Allah, Absolute Oneness,
Allah, the Everlasting Sustainer of all.
He has not given birth and was not born.
And no one is comparable to Him.'

Frequent repetition of this, and reflection on its meanings, builds up certainty in the mumin about the truth of Allah, and protects him against giving credence to ideas that might lead to an outlook on life which is at variance to the real situation.

Let us return to the question I mentioned at the outset and its implication that the Decree might contain injustice. Cruelty and injustice can be ascribed to human actions, because a person may act against someone without justification and may relish causing suffering to others. He may without good reason inflict injury on someone, by the tongue or by physical or financial actions. Such actions can be described as cruel and unjust.

Yet inflicting injury on others is not always deemed wrong. If a man commits a wrong action, then we expect and demand that he be either punished, or forgiven, but not left to carry on with impunity. A person or society which fails to punish criminals is itself considered corrupt and unjust.

Allah, may He be exalted above all human attributes, is entirely perfect in His Justice, indeed justice belongs to Him and it is one of His Attributes, so the very existence of justice emanates from Him and He is the Possessor of all justice. His actions are, by definition, the working-out of the ultimate justice, and the judgment in the Akhira is the completion of justice.

When we think carefully about justice, it necessarily reverts to Allah, subhanahu wa ta'ala, because, on close examination, we humans are incapable of absolute justice in even the most insignificant of judgments, let alone important ones. So for justice to exist, we must recognise Allah as the perfect Possessor of it, otherwise we will end up negating its existence altogether, as nihilists do, saying there is no such thing.

With our knowledge of Allah's perfect possession of justice firmly established, we may look at the Decree properly. Allah, may He be exalted, says in His Book:

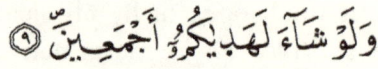

If He had wished,
He could have guided every one of you.

Justice of the Decree and Free Will

And in a well-known Hadith reported by Abdullah ibn Mas'ud, the Messenger of Allah, sallallahu 'alayhi wa sallam, said, "The creation of each of you takes place by being brought together in your mother's womb for forty days as a drop, then for a similar period as a clot, then for a similar period as a lump of flesh. Then the angel is sent to it to breathe the Ruh into it and is ordered to dictate four things: its provision, its lifespan, its actions and whether it will be in the Fire or the Garden."

So, by the Decree of Allah, we are destined for the Fire or the Garden – and may Allah re-unite us all in the Garden. When we proceed from the certain knowledge that all justice belongs to Allah and He is perfect and complete in His Justice, then the destiny of those who are created for the Fire reveals itself, not as a matter of doubt or objection, but as a warning to us and an incentive to ask Allah to make us among those of the Garden, and a motivation to call people to the Garden and do things with the intention of pleasing Allah. Allah's sending people to the Fire cannot be described as cruel or unjust because that would presuppose they did not deserve it, and He says:

مَّن كَانَ يُرِيدُ ٱلْعَاجِلَةَ عَجَّلْنَا لَهُۥ فِيهَا مَا نَشَآءُ لِمَن نُّرِيدُ ثُمَّ جَعَلْنَا لَهُۥ جَهَنَّمَ يَصْلَىٰهَا مَذْمُومًا مَّدْحُورًا ۝ وَمَنْ أَرَادَ ٱلْءَاخِرَةَ وَسَعَىٰ لَهَا سَعْيَهَا وَهُوَ مُؤْمِنٌ فَأُو۟لَٰٓئِكَ كَانَ سَعْيُهُم مَّشْكُورًا ۝

> As for anyone who desires this fleeting existence,
> We hasten in it whatever We will
> to whomever We want.
> Then We will consign him to Hell
> where he will roast, reviled and driven out.
> But as for anyone who desires the Akhira,
> and strives for it with the striving it deserves,
> being a mumin,
> the striving of such people
> will be gratefully acknowledged.

So each of us is created with the actions that will take us either to the Fire or the Garden, but it is people's desire that sends them to what they go to.

Without wrong action and its punishment, and without right action and its reward, justice would have no meaning and we would not be able to know our Lord in His Attribute of Justice. This is not meant as a rational, apologistic justification, since the motives of Allah, subhanahu wa ta'ala, are far above needing justification. It is we who hope for justification, and we who fear the consequences of our own injustice.

While we are firm in recognising the justice and meaning of the Fire or the Garden, we may nevertheless find ourselves feeling sad and concerned when we contemplate the possible fate of people we may have grown to love, such as non-Muslim parents, siblings, children or friends. It is important that we are clear and correct when we face up to this situation.

Justice of the Decree and Free Will

Firstly it should be remembered that the final judgment on any individual remains hidden in the foreknowledge of Allah, with the exception of what has been revealed to us about certain people in the past. Having said that, there is no doubt whatsoever that the kuffar will be in the Fire. This we have to accept with gravity and obedience.

Allah says, subhanahu wa ta'ala:

وَالَّذِينَ كَفَرُوا وَكَذَّبُوا بِآيَاتِنَا أُوْلَٰئِكَ أَصْحَابُ النَّارِ هُمْ فِيهَا خَالِدُونَ ۝

> But those who are kafir and deny Our Signs
> are the Companions of the Fire,
> remaining in it timelessly, for ever.

Furthermore, we cannot evade this situation by trying to redefine the meaning of the word kafir and claiming that it excludes Christians and Jews because they are People of the Book. The Christians and Jews who make false claims about Allah are judged to be kuffar, and to say otherwise would be to deny Allah's words in the Qur'an.

Allah ta'ala says in His Mighty Book:

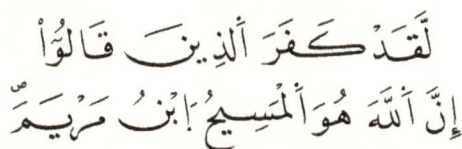

Those who say, "Allah is the Messiah,
son of Maryam," are kafir.

And:

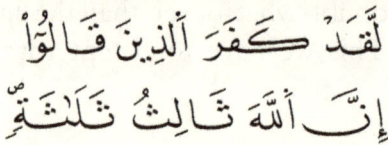

Those who say, "Allah is the third of three,"
are kafirun.

Notwithstanding, we must remember that we do not know the ultimate judgment with Allah on any particular individual, or what belief they will end up dying on, and Christians, especially these days, may conceivably reject parts of their own doctrine, especially the trinity and the divinity of Jesus, peace be upon him. Or they may be so far from their religion that they do not think about such things. And they may instinctively avoid thinking about it.

We find that Allah says in His Noble Book:

إِنَّ ٱلَّذِينَ ءَامَنُوا۟ وَٱلَّذِينَ هَادُوا۟ وَٱلنَّصَٰرَىٰ وَٱلصَّٰبِـِٔينَ مَنْ ءَامَنَ بِٱللَّهِ وَٱلْيَوْمِ ٱلْءَاخِرِ وَعَمِلَ صَٰلِحًا فَلَهُمْ أَجْرُهُمْ عِندَ رَبِّهِمْ وَلَا خَوْفٌ عَلَيْهِمْ وَلَا هُمْ يَحْزَنُونَ ۝

Justice of the Decree and Free Will

> Those with iman, those who are Jews,
> and the Christians and Sabaeans,
> all who have iman in Allah
> and the Last Day and act rightly,
> will have their reward with their Lord.
> They will feel no fear and will know no sorrow.

This is why we avoid casting judgment on individuals unless evidence demands that we speak. Rather, we are suspended between fear on people's behalf and hope that Allah will look kindly on them. It is our concern for people that moves us to ask Allah on their behalf, and this may be the means by which Allah changes their hearts. Look at the behaviour of our Prophet Muhammad, sallallahu 'alayhi wa sallam, with his uncle who refused to accept Islam even though the Prophet was with him. He, sallallahu 'alayhi wa sallam, remained kind to him to the end and kept trying to persuade him to say the Shahada.

So, what is the cure for doubt about the justice of the Decree? In Surat al-Anbiya, Allah, subhanahu wa ta'ala, says:

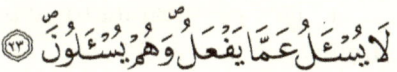

> He will not be questioned about what He does,
> but they will be questioned.

The remedy for doubts about the justice of the Decree is not some kind of all-conclusive intellectual argument. It is to remember that we will be questioned and He, may He be exalted, will not be questioned. He is the Lord and we are the slaves. And the cure is to keep the company of people who are firm in that.

* * *

Given that our destinies are preordained and we are created for the Fire or the Garden, where then does free will come into it and what is the point of making any decisions or being careful about one's actions?

Take the example of two men. The first man, suspecting that his destiny is already written for him – thinking things will end up however they end up – or simply living out his life without any reflection at all – says to himself that he need not worry about his actions, or he merely does not reflect on them. Reposing in this state, he becomes negligent of any responsibilities and duties to others and himself, and lets himself go. Doing anything worthwhile becomes harder and harder for him. He gets into a routine of neglect to himself and others, until it becomes habitual for him to harm himself and others without even noticing it. His indolence and lack of meaningful activity damage himself, his family and his society.

The second man, in response to the realisation that his destiny is already written for him, and wishing for a good destiny and fearing a bad one, decides to do everything he possibly can to get to the Garden. He builds up good actions wherever he can, and in doing so, good actions become easier and easier for him. He becomes accustomed to being good to himself and others until he barely notices that he is doing so, and that itself is added to his balance. He is given extra energy because he helps others and is not concerned about himself, and his family and the people he comes into contact with are affected by the baraka of his activities.

What we see by these two examples is that, instead of free will and destiny being opposed, they are in fact one process. It is by a person's acts of will that their destiny is shaped. Both men act, but the actions of the one are very different from the actions of the other. One set of actions proceed from a sick heart, the other from a sound heart.

It is Allah, may He be exalted, Who possesses all Will, and that Will is exercised through the drives, decisions and aspirations of humans and all creatures, and by the tendency of all objects, even inanimate ones, to fulfil their purpose. As Ibn 'Arabi says, Allah governs the universe from inside the universe – and not by "divine intervention".

Going back to the ayat mentioned earlier, we see that Allah says: "As for anyone who desires this fleeting existence." That is the true definition of fatalists and predeterminists. Anyone who claims to himself that it doesn't matter what we do, is actually saying so as a cover for their desire of this world.

'Umar ibn al-Khattab, radiyallahu 'anhu, was told about a group of people calling themselves the Mutawakkilun

– the people who rely on Allah – and staying in the mosque allowing people to bring them food. He went to see them and said, "You are not Mutawakkilun, you are Muta'akkilun – people who expect others to feed them. Get out of the mosque and do something useful with your lives."

Allah ta'ala says in Surat at-Takwir:

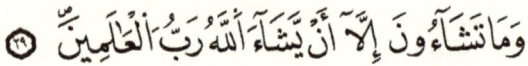

But you will not will unless Allah wills,
the Lord of all the Worlds.

This may elude us in our daily lives because our will is so central to our own identity that it can be difficult to see it as being the means by which Allah manifests His Will. But look at creation in general and reflect on the fact that we are merely part of it, and you will recognise this, until such time that Allah gives us the certainty of direct experience, either in this world or the Next.

This is not a knowledge that can be captured in words and put in a book. It can only be contained in the heart, and for that the heart must be kept clear, otherwise the knowledge will refuse to reside in it. It is by keeping company with people of certainty and avoiding people of doubt and scepticism, and by acting with the intention of pleasing Allah, that our own certainty develops and we are eased into the station which we seek to attain.

LANGUAGE AND KNOWLEDGE

Allah ta'ala says in His Noble Book:

وَإِذْ قَالَ رَبُّكَ لِلْمَلَٰٓئِكَةِ إِنِّى جَاعِلٌ فِى ٱلْأَرْضِ خَلِيفَةً قَالُوٓا۟ أَتَجْعَلُ فِيهَا مَن يُفْسِدُ فِيهَا وَيَسْفِكُ ٱلدِّمَآءَ وَنَحْنُ نُسَبِّحُ بِحَمْدِكَ وَنُقَدِّسُ لَكَ قَالَ إِنِّىٓ أَعْلَمُ مَا لَا تَعْلَمُونَ ۝ وَعَلَّمَ ءَادَمَ ٱلْأَسْمَآءَ كُلَّهَا ثُمَّ عَرَضَهُمْ عَلَى ٱلْمَلَٰٓئِكَةِ فَقَالَ أَنۢبِـُٔونِى بِأَسْمَآءِ هَٰٓؤُلَآءِ إِن كُنتُمْ صَٰدِقِينَ ۝ قَالُوا۟ سُبْحَٰنَكَ لَا عِلْمَ لَنَآ إِلَّا مَا عَلَّمْتَنَآ إِنَّكَ أَنتَ ٱلْعَلِيمُ ٱلْحَكِيمُ ۝

> When your Lord said to the angels,
> 'I am putting a khalif on the earth,'
> they said, 'Why put on it
> one who will cause corruption on it
> and shed blood
> when we glorify You with praise
> and proclaim Your purity?'
> He said, 'I know what you do not know.'
>
> He taught Adam the names of all things.
> Then He arrayed them before the angels and said,
> 'Tell me the names of these
> if you are telling the truth.'
>
> They said, 'Glory be to You! We have no knowledge
> except what You have taught us.
> You are the All-Knowing, the All-Wise.'

These famous and magnificent ayats and the ones that follow them indicate two important matters.

They demonstrate that language is the factor that sets man above even the angels. What was revealed to Adam, 'alayhi salam, were the names of things. Having the vocabulary to identify the features of existence sets man apart.

The Qur'an is the Word of Allah. It was not sent as a set of exercises, a diet, a map, or a set of ritual practices, although it contains aspects of all those things. It is words. It is not even writing. It is Qur'an – recitation. The tongue is the highest of man's outward physical faculties and we are called to Allah by words. We also call on Him using words.

But the tongue can also be man's downfall. Mu'adh bin Jabal reported that the Messenger of Allah, sallallahu 'alayhi wa sallam, said to him, "The root of this matter is Islam and its pillar is Salat." Then he asked, "Shall I tell you of that which holds these things?" I said: "Yes, Messenger of Allah." So he took hold of his tongue and said, "Keep this in control."

Qadi 'Iyad says, "The Prophet's pre-eminence in eloquence and fluency of speech is well known. He was fluent, skilful in debate, very concise, clear in expression, lucid, used sound meanings and was free from affectation."

He was also described as, "Sweet in speech, distinct, without using too few or too many words. It was as if his speech consisted of threaded pearls. He had a loud voice which was very melodious, may Allah bless him and grant him peace."

Speech is our prime physical faculty as human beings, and we must treat it as such.

As well as being the means of Revelation, speech is the door to belief. The first pillar of Islam is the Shahada. If you have never uttered the Shahada in your life, you are, in the Law, not a Muslim.

Words matter. And it is one of the signs of a believer

that he understands that. Conversely, the kuffar, when it suits their political aims, claim that words do not matter and that you can say whatever you like. They call this freedom of speech. But every people and society sets limits on what can be said, including them. Especially them. The taboos and political correctness of the kuffar are an embarrassment even to themselves.

There is a long section in Qadi 'Iyad's seminal work, Ash-Shifa, describing the terrible judgment on anyone who says anything bad about the Messenger of Allah, may Allah bless him and grant him peace. This is because nothing good could come out of a person who says such things and does not repent.

What we say matters very much, and every Muslim must make it his or her business to consider their speech and use good words. This is not to suggest that we need to use complicated language or have large vocabularies. But we do need to develop an awareness about what we say and how we say it.

This includes the way we address one another. The Messenger of Allah, may Allah bless him and grant him peace, disliked the use of demeaning nicknames and used instead the noble names his Companions had been given. He did not call anybody using truncated forms of their Muslim names, like 'Abdul', 'Mo', or 'Dicky'. These things bring people low, whereas a name like Abdulbasir or Siddiq brings a person high because it reminds them of their reality. Calling somebody by the additional title of 'Pir', or 'Mawlana', which means master, or 'Shaykh', or 'Hajj', which acknowledges that the person once left everything to go to the House of Allah – these are beautiful acts of courtesy which elevate the speaker and the one addressed.

I ought to mention that the appellation of "brother", in the way it is commonly used today, does not belong to this category at all. It is disliked, because it tries to bring the person down to our own level, whereas it is preferable to assume that others are above us. 'Brother', if used as a name to address an individual, has no precedent in Islam until recently, and does not occur in any of the classical narrations. It is true that we are brothers and sisters in Islam, and that one may address an assembly as such; or we might say, "our dear brother so-and-so;" but there is a great difference between that and saying "How are you, brother?" It is probable that this disliked practice found its way to us through the socialism that pervaded the Arab peoples in the 20th century and continues to leave its overgrown moustaches, shaved chins and national disasters across the Muslim world.

Rather than reducing our names to monosyllables, we can explain them to non-Muslims with whom we are on good terms, if we wish good for them and wish them to have access to the possibility of knowing their own reality.

Sadly, at this stage in history, language and general speech are in decline. This is not a nostalgic or sentimental statement. Allah mentions numerous times in Qur'an the rise of powerful civilisations and their subsequent decline and destruction. Societies progress in cycles: they rise to a peak, then sink towards decay and disappearance. Language reflects this, and the proof that our language is in decline is in our literature.

Just as art has undergone a process of simplification and abstraction in the past hundred years, so too has language. It is not that brilliance no longer exists; it is that the tools have gradually gone missing and we are left with very few. The language of modern classics is slick, reduced and minimalist, where it used to be rich and sophisticated. This is not a value judgment or a preference, it is a technical statement. There has been a decline in vocabulary.

Not only does language enable us to express our thoughts, but the ability to articulate is inextricably linked with the ability to think. Acclaimed author and Carnegie Prize winner Geraldine McCaughrean, commenting on the 'dumbing-down' of children's books, said:

"Since when has one generation ever doubted and pitied the next so much that it decides not to burden them with the full package of the English language but to feed them only a restricted diet of simple words? The worst and most wicked outcome of all, would be that we deliberately and wantonly create an underclass of citizens with a small but functional vocabulary: easy to manipulate and lacking in the means to reason their way out of subjugation, because you need words to be able to think for yourself."

While we may not be able to stem this sad tide for everyone, we can certainly be conscious of our own speech and do our best to choose good and elevating words.

* * *

In the ayats I mentioned at the beginning, once Allah, subhanahu wa ta'ala, had told the angels that He knew what they did not know, He then ordered Adam to tell them the names of things. Then He said to the angels:

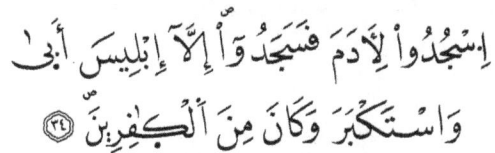

'Prostrate to Adam!'
and they prostrated, with the exception of Iblis.
He refused and was arrogant
and was one of the kafirun.

The first question the angels had asked, when they discovered that Allah was putting man on the earth as khalif, was, "Why put on it one who will cause corruption on it and shed blood when we glorify You with praise and proclaim Your purity?" In other words, "Why choose a misbehaving creature like man, and not a species of being that is free of wrong actions?"

On the face of it, this recalls the sentiment of people who say, "When will we stop all these wars, when will everyone start behaving at last and when will wrong actions somehow cease so that we can live in peace?" On the face of it, this seems reasonable. But it is based on not knowing.

Allah replies to the angels:

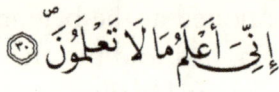

I know what you do not know.

And, because they are incapable of disobedience, they immediately reply:

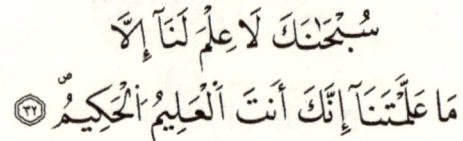

'Glory be to You! We have no knowledge
except what You have taught us.
You are the All-Knowing, the All-Wise.'

When they are corrected by Allah, they submit instantly by saying, "We have no knowledge." Their humility is to accept that there are things they do not know.

That is the position of the Muslim.

Then, when the angels were asked to prostrate to someone with greater knowledge than them, they all did, except Iblis, who refused and was arrogant.

That is the position of the kafir. Even once he has been shown that he does not know everything, he refuses to accept it. His arrogance is arrogance in the face of greater knowledge. The kuffar believe that they will eventually know everything, and that their knowledge can eventually be all-encompassing.

But the truth is, it is they who are encompassed. They – and we – will only ever know that small portion of things which we have been decreed to know.

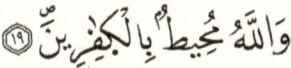

Allah encompasses the kafireen.

This 'Muhit' is encompassing in the sense of a wall around something, but Allah also has the name of Al-Wasi'a, encompassing in the sense of knowledge, which is most often connected in Qur'an with His name Al-'Alim, the Knower:

Allah is All-Encompassing, All-Knowing.

The primal kufr is that they presume to know, or to be able to know, everything there is to know, thus arrogating Allah's attributes to themselves.

This reflects a view of knowledge which sees it as items of information. It explains the fantasy that computers could eventually collect so much information that they would begin to act like humans and even develop consciousness. It is only possible to believe that if one ignores the very thing that makes us human.

What in fact is happening, as computers get more sophisticated and man becomes more captivated by them, is not that they become more like him but that he gradually becomes more like them: unable to act on any spiritual conviction. The intelligence of man is becoming artificial.

The kuffar, believing they are acquiring more knowledge, are becoming less able to properly explore the landscapes of thought and reflection, because they are looking for a knowledge they can encompass, and not for a knowledge that encompasses them.

The Muslim is saved from that because he has tied himself to the Prayer and the Hajj and the Fast, and he has fear of Allah and hope in Allah, knowledges which are not information-based. They are states of heart. And it is by man's heart that his destiny unfolds, whether Muslim or kafir. The kuffar do not know this, and even when they glimpse it, they try somehow to possess it and make it 'their own', whereas the Muslim knows that iman is a gift constantly pouring out from Allah.

RIBA AND MADNESS

Allah, subhanahu wa ta'ala, the Creator of us and our actions, says in His Noble Book:

$$\text{ٱلَّذِينَ يَأْكُلُونَ ٱلرِّبَوٰاْ لَا يَقُومُونَ إِلَّا كَمَا يَقُومُ ٱلَّذِي يَتَخَبَّطُهُ ٱلشَّيْطَٰنُ مِنَ ٱلْمَسِّ ذَٰلِكَ بِأَنَّهُمْ قَالُوٓاْ إِنَّمَا ٱلْبَيْعُ مِثْلُ ٱلرِّبَوٰاْ وَأَحَلَّ ٱللَّهُ ٱلْبَيْعَ وَحَرَّمَ ٱلرِّبَوٰاْ}$$

> Those who practise riba will not rise from the grave
> except as someone driven mad by Shaytan's touch.
> That is because they say, 'Trade is the same as riba.'
> But Allah has permitted trade
> and He has forbidden riba.

What is this 'riba' which drives people and whole societies mad?

The Imam of Madinah, Malik, radiyallahu 'anhu, has in his Muwatta: "Yahya related to me from Malik that he had heard that receipts were given to people in the time of Marwan ibn al-Hakam for the produce of the market at al-Jar. People bought and sold the receipts among themselves before they had taken actual delivery of the goods. Zayd ibn Thabit and one of the Companions of the Messenger of Allah, sallallahu 'alayhi wa sallam, went to Marwan, and Zayd said, 'Marwan, are you making riba halal?' He said, 'A'udhu billah! What do you mean?' He replied, 'These receipts which people buy and sell before they take delivery of the goods.' So Marwan sent guards to round them up and take the receipts from people and return them to their owners."

From this and numerous other accounts we know that riba is more than just "interest". It can be an unfair or uncertain delay between a sale and delivery, or between delivery and payment, indeed any unjust increase in a financial transaction. And it can be inherent uncertainty in transactions, as with the receipts of al-Jar.

Sometimes such an increase can be dressed as convenience, like when 'Ubayd Abu Salih said, "I sold some drapery to the people of Dar Nakhla on credit. Then I wanted to go to Kufa, so they suggested that I reduce the price for them and they would pay me immediately. I asked Zayd ibn Thabit about it and he said, 'I order you not to accept increase or to allow it to anybody.'"

This very precise, discerning and clean atmosphere in

the Madinah of the Companions contrasts starkly with our situation today. Not only are modern transactions full of deceit; the very currency in which we conduct them decreases with the same dishonesty. Like the receipts of al-Jar, our money is a token of no intrinsic value. It is only money because, like the people at the market of Al-Jar, we have all agreed to use it.

We have grown up in societies where money is debased into something our ancestors would not recognise. Inflation and the pumping of money into the financial system by banks and governments are overt riba, because it is unlawful to manufacture instruments of exchange out of nothing and then spend them.

Money has changed from being worth something in itself, like gold or silver, firstly into paper tokens, then into just the numbers in bank balances. And that transformation has allowed money to be created out of nothing – all the time, continuously – and to decrease in its buying power.

All of this has produced a world in which everything appears to get gradually more expensive. Our financial experience, from birth onwards, is that "prices go up". It is actually an illusion, since the real value of a thing remains the same, provided the thing remains the same. But the numerical effect of inflation produces such a powerful illusion that we are conditioned to think of things getting more expensive. We live in a world of *seeming* increase in price, whose corollary is *seeming* decrease in what is available to us, down to our very sustenance. Living itself seems to get more difficult. We grow up and live in a slowly closing vice.

Economics has become about, and obsessed with, the idea of "growth". If there is no "growth" in a Western economy, it is almost a national disaster. And the populations of these countries are not growing, so there is no rational explanation for it. Rather it is because everything has the *appearance* of getting more expensive and less available, so it seems as if there has to be more and more money around, just to keep a nation's head above water. There is an unexamined compulsion to make everything "grow". Humans, in other words, experience everything as shrinking, due to the criminal creation of money out of nothing. So they insist on everything growing and expanding, just to counteract it. Countries, cities and businesses are considered worthless junk if they are not growing. And the money shrinks. And shrinks.

This can be seen as the root cause of man's destruction of our planet, since he has to eat up and consume things without reason, driven by a pathological urge to counter the shrivelling money, without even understanding what drives him. As long as we seek a technical solution to the ecological disaster and fail to see its financial origins, we will not stop it.

Islam forbids, in the most severe terms, every kind of deceitful transaction and the debasement of currency. The punishments for corrupting currency are frightening, and rightly so, because debasing currency brings forth a delusional society of people bent on destroying the world and each other, all for a growth which is but an illusion.

For the small man on the street, the shrinking nature of his money, the slowly closing vice, and the fact that his life has become a solely financial project, all have a more immediate effect. It is slowly driving him mad.

Allah, subhanahu wa ta'ala, says:

$$\text{الَّذِينَ يَأْكُلُونَ الرِّبَوٰا۟ لَا يَقُومُونَ إِلَّا كَمَا يَقُومُ الَّذِى يَتَخَبَّطُهُ الشَّيْطَانُ مِنَ الْمَسِّ}$$

Those who practise riba will not rise from the grave except as someone driven mad by Shaytan's touch.

It is by the light of Allah's rulings that the cause of an evil is revealed.

It is by the light of the Messenger of Allah that the cure is revealed.

The discourse around Islam is the wrong one. The Deen has not come to this or any country to stop people going to the pub or make women cover their hair or, God forbid, their faces. And certainly not to suggest to lonely and vulnerable people via the Internet to kill themselves while taking as many innocents with them as they can. The opposite is true. What we have is transmitted openly, face to uncovered face, and brings life and hope and health, understanding and meaning. It allows people to understand why it is right to behave with courtesy, generosity and justice. And it allows people to understand the financial pressure they experience and do something about it.

We face a task much more important than petty moral issues – much more essential to the lives of everyone, and much more interesting. We, the Muslims, know that wrong money and wrong transactions and wrong economics are contrary to the created pattern, and we know the shape of what is right. It is real currency, it is the equitable contracts of the fiqh. It is being straight. None of this ever goes out of date. It is futuristic, because we are languishing in a time of financial decay which will not go on for ever, and upon which people will look back with horror and disgust, wondering how such a dark age and such a primitive society could ever have existed and how humanity survived it.

All this needs to be said publicly, especially when we are asked about terrorism. The causes of terrorism can be found described by Dostoevsky and other deconstructors of nihilism. We Muslims have a more urgent message. We say:

ٱلَّذِينَ يَأْكُلُونَ ٱلرِّبَوٰاْ لَا يَقُومُونَ إِلَّا كَمَا يَقُومُ ٱلَّذِى يَتَخَبَّطُهُ ٱلشَّيْطَٰنُ مِنَ ٱلْمَسِّ ذَٰلِكَ بِأَنَّهُمْ قَالُوٓاْ إِنَّمَا ٱلْبَيْعُ مِثْلُ ٱلرِّبَوٰاْ وَأَحَلَّ ٱللَّهُ ٱلْبَيْعَ وَحَرَّمَ ٱلرِّبَوٰاْ

Those who practise riba will not rise from the grave except as someone driven mad by Shaytan's touch. That is because they say, 'Trade is the same as riba.'
But Allah has permitted trade
and He has forbidden riba.

It would be wrong to suggest that speaking out on this is the only cure. It is the beginning of the long-term cure which will involve establishing an alternative. But the patient is urgently ill. People's mental wellbeing is in crisis.

The Messenger of Allah, sallallahu 'alayhi wa sallam, and his Companions, kept company with each other and ate together. The Muslims have always disliked eating alone. We are often encouraged to invite each other to our houses to eat, and it can never be said enough. In the adverse financial climate I have described, being alone and not seeing other Muslims is disastrous.

I am not talking about visiting and spending time with your family. While that is necessary and hopefully a pleasure and a source of goodness, it is not what I am talking about. I am talking about making it your habit to visit, invite, spend time with and do business with other Muslims to whom you have no blood relation, both here and further afield.

Go and visit your brothers or sisters in Islam, for the sake of gaining the blessings of Allah from where you do not know.

Visit someone you have not visited. Invite someone

you have not invited. At work, suggest to your Muslim co-worker that you eat together, and even pray together if it is possible. Break the ice.

Invite Muslims to your house. Inviting people is what makes your house ready to receive people. How many a house has been made ready for the coming guest!

Travel. Travel to see other Muslims. See what their concerns are. See how you might be able to contribute and help. I don't mean financially, I mean in ways which you will only discover by going out and visiting.

Meet each other in public, in groups. When people see the Muslims together and their courtesy with each other and their light, some of them will think to themselves, "I want to have what those people have."

TECHNOLOGY AND THE ENVIRONMENT

إِنَّ فِى خَلْقِ ٱلسَّمَٰوَٰتِ وَٱلْأَرْضِ وَٱخْتِلَٰفِ ٱلَّيْلِ وَٱلنَّهَارِ وَٱلْفُلْكِ ٱلَّتِى تَجْرِى فِى ٱلْبَحْرِ بِمَا يَنفَعُ ٱلنَّاسَ وَمَآ أَنزَلَ ٱللَّهُ مِنَ ٱلسَّمَآءِ مِن مَّآءٍ

In the creation of the heavens and earth,
and the alternation of the night and day,
and the ships which sail the seas to people's benefit,
and the water which Allah sends down from the sky –

Recently I heard a Muslim say that technology since the Industrial Revolution is "secular", by which he meant not part of Islam and not befitting believing people. He added to this his rejection of social media for children and other complaints about digital technology.

It reminded me of other people who say they wish to escape the technical society and set up rural lives, back in nature.

While these are understandable sentiments, given the oppressive grip technology has on us, they indicate a misunderstanding of the nature of technology and its delineation. It is important that we have a sound basic understanding of what it is, since we are immersed in it.

Technology is defined as the application of scientific knowledge to practical matters, as well as the machinery and equipment based on that knowledge. Science, in this context, is the intellectual and practical activity encompassing the systematic study of the structure and behaviour of the physical and natural world through observation and experiment.

In other words, science is observing and trying things out in the world to build up an ordered body of knowledge about it. Technology is using that knowledge to make machines and systems. Or to put it simply: man has noticed that certain things tend to happen, so he invents and develops things, and they are technology.

The wheel is technology. The process by which it came about is lost in the mists of time. Weapons are technology and have been subject to an improvement process since history began, a process which has itself shaped historical events.

The Muslims have never opted out of any of this, and that includes our first community, who used weapons and other forms of technology. Furthermore, technology like boats and weapons are mentioned by Allah in the Qur'an, such as the ships which sail the seas to people's benefit as mentioned in the ayat I began with, and in Surat al-Muminun:

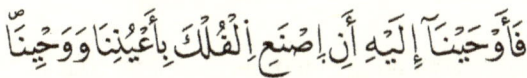

> We revealed to him: 'Build the ship
> under Our supervision and as We reveal.'

This and the other sublime ayat from Surat al-Baqara provide a complete basis for understanding the very essence of technology. What is extraordinary in the first ayat is that Allah places man's ships in among a series of natural phenomena: the creation of the heavens and earth, the alternation of the night and day, the ships which sail the seas to people's benefit, and the water which He sends down from the sky.

In the other ayat He, subhanahu wa ta'ala, informs us that He "revealed" to Sayyiduna Nuh, 'alayhi salam, to build the ship "under His supervision and as He revealed." In other words, knowledge of the ship was divinely uncovered in Sayyiduna Nuh, both its concept and the process of building it.

And indeed other ancient man-made phenomena such as bread, which comes from grinding an unremarkable looking seed, mixing its flour with water and letting it rise, then baking it – while it is not impossible that this was discovered by observation, trial and error or some kind of evolutionary piece of good luck, it accords more with common sense that it was a matter of inspiration.

Technology is clearly part of man's nature and is beneficial. It cannot be written off.

But it does not take a scientist to tell us that in this age we live in, technology has got out of hand.

Not only is technology playing a major part in the hurtling destruction of the planet, it also has a devastating psychological impact on an already atomised social fabric. It provides unnaturally easy access to imagery and information which has no actual bearing on our physical lives, thus stimulating us to an extreme in matters we cannot control. News technology tells us all day long about selected events we cannot and will not influence, and social media technology has contributed towards, but not exclusively caused, the withdrawal of humans from real social interactions, displacing them gradually into a virtual realm where anything can and will be said with impunity, and causing a rapid devolution in their ability to respond to real human stimuli in the here and now.

The drive for vast technological projects, fuelled by and even caused by the need to satiate the practitioners of riba, has destroyed large tracts of the earth. True silence in the countryside, true darkness at night, truly pure water – all are receding before the technological surge. The technology of food production has wiped out huge areas of forest and decimated insects and wildlife and oceans.

There is clearly something wrong in the relationship man now has with the technology he has made. It has gone from the usefulness of ships, to the destruction of the oceans, now awash with plastic debris, shipping containers and toxic waste.

The great German thinker Heidegger went some way towards understanding man's relationship with technology. Interestingly, he described the way man looks at the world in terms of unveiling, or 'Entbergen' – unconcealing. But for us Muslims, our direct access to the guidance of the One who created it give us an immeasurable advantage over even remarkable thinkers like him.

It is not a question of trying to backpedal to a time before man made a fundamental mistake by releasing some particularly demonic technology. Such claims have been made by many serious scientists, such as Dr Natasha Winters and Higgins Kelley, food scientists who, along with others, claim that the act of cultivation itself was a mistake and imply that our aim should be to revert to a precultivated food supply. Not only is this impossible, it ignores the essential nature of the human being to derive benefit from his own aptitudes and the environment around him.

* * *

I will mention three things in regard to our attitude to technology. Firstly, **riba**. Secondly, **'aqida**. And thirdly, **discrimination.**

Firstly, then, there is the matter of riba. The total domination of riba finance under every single stone and upon every single grain of sand and dust and in almost every corner of the human mind can be seen as the prime mover in the proliferation of destructive technology. As mentioned previously, Allah the Exalted says in his book:

$$\text{اَلَّذِينَ يَأْكُلُونَ ٱلرِّبَوٰاْ لَا يَقُومُونَ إِلَّا كَمَا يَقُومُ ٱلَّذِي يَتَخَبَّطُهُ ٱلشَّيْطَٰنُ مِنَ ٱلْمَسِّ}$$

Those who practise riba will not rise from the grave except as someone driven mad by Shaytan's touch.

This madness of riba is evident in the truly demonic partnership of high technology and high finance. Scientists have proposed a new geological epoch called the 'Anthropocene', in which human thought – science, in other words, and the technology that it spawns – has started to have more than just an insignificant impact on the Earth's geology and ecosystems. Various dates have been proposed for the beginning of this epoch, the earliest being the introduction of agriculture. But as the environmental thinker Fazlun Khalid has pointed out, the age of environmental disaster started not with the Agricultural or indeed Industrial Revolution, but with the formal introduction of riba in the Christian society which, in collaboration with the Jewish, went on to dominate global socio-political development.

> "A working group, reporting to a congress of geologists in 2016, said that, 'in its considered opinion, the Anthropocene epoch began in 1950 – the start of the era of nuclear bomb tests, disposable plastics and the human population boom.' Other dates such as 1800 were suggested, as this was the time when the Industrial Revolution was beginning to take a grip, but I think there is another date that needs to be considered which profoundly changed the nature of the human relationship with the Earth, and this was when interest was legitimised by Henry VIII in 1545. This was the event that eventually led to the creation of the Bank of England in 1694, enshrining the magical fractional reserve banking system which conjures money out of thin air and has kept the entire planetary population in its thrall ever since."

The Earth, then, has been subject to epochs of formation and change, and this now is the epoch in which man has become the instrument of its depletion. In case anybody considers this an exaggeration, the IPBES Report on Global Biodiversity, published in 2019 and backed by the United Nations, tells us that while the Earth has always suffered from the actions of humans through history, over the past 50 years, these scratches have become deep scars.

To paraphrase the report, between 1980 and 2000, 100 million hectares of tropical forest were lost, more than four times the area of the United Kingdom. Faring worse than forests are wetlands, with only 13% of those present in 1700 still in existence in the year 2000. Our cities have expanded rapidly, with urban areas doubling since 1992. All this human activity is killing species in greater numbers than ever before. According to the global assessment, an average of around 25% of animals and plants are now threatened. Global trends in insect populations are not known but rapid declines in some locations have also been well documented, such as the Krefeld Entomological Survey in 2016, which discovered a 75% reduction in insect biomass in German conservation areas over the preceding 27 years. All this suggests around a million species now face extinction within decades, a rate of destruction tens to hundreds of times higher than the average over the past ten million years.

Man continues to think he can somehow fix all this. But it is the Muslims who have the instruction manual for the world and all that is on it, and the first thing it says when you open the book is:

يَٰٓأَيُّهَا ٱلَّذِينَ ءَامَنُوا۟ ٱتَّقُوا۟ ٱللَّهَ وَذَرُوا۟ مَا بَقِىَ مِنَ ٱلرِّبَوٰٓا۟ إِن كُنتُم مُّؤْمِنِينَ ۝

> You who have iman! have taqwa of Allah
> and forgo any remaining riba
> if you are muminun.

It is commonly held that if we can apply science cleverly enough and legislate morally good science stringently and quickly enough, things will become "sustainable" and all will be saved.

This is based on two fundamental misconceptions that arise from wrong 'aqida. The first is that the world can be sustainable. On the contrary, the world is inherently unsustainable. It is in a constant process of deterioration, and it is Allah alone who sustains it and is Himself Self-Sustaining.

Allah ta'ala says in Surat ar-Rahman:

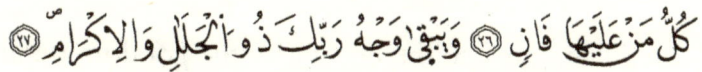

> Everything on the Earth is in annihilation;
> but the Face of your Lord remains,
> Master of Majesty and Generosity.

It is Allah, the Exalted, who keeps the creation in any balance it may have, and it is He who forms the epochs. The Anthropocene epoch, if such a thing exists, is but another manifestation of Allah's power. When one society goes beyond the bounds, He replaces it with another.

$$\text{أَوَلَمْ يَسِيرُوا فِي الْأَرْضِ فَيَنظُرُوا كَيْفَ كَانَ عَاقِبَةُ الَّذِينَ مِن قَبْلِهِمْ}$$

> Have they not travelled in the earth
> and seen the final fate of those before them?

A firm understanding of these matters lies in a correct 'aqida, and this is acquired by transmission from those people to whom Allah has granted it. They must be protected, honoured and visited.

Finally, there is the discrimination of Rasul, sallallahu 'alayhi wa sallam, in entering upon the day and upon any thing, a du'a which we use in every matter and especially in the physical means by which we live our lives:

"Oh Allah, give me the benefit of the good in it and protect me from the bad in it."

Through constant use and reflection, this becomes a state of being, whereby the primary faculty with which we discern the world around us becomes the heart, with its limitless capacity to discriminate between what is good and what is bad.

To summarise, our manifesto for the rescue of the environment consists of insisting on the abolition of riba and its replacement with lawful finance; protecting and accompanying the possessors of correct 'aqida; and the mighty du'a of Rasul, sallallahu 'alayhi wa sallam.

We ask Allah, to give us the benefit of the good in technology and protect us from the bad in it. We ask Him, subhanah, to give us the benefit of the good in our food and drink and protect us from the bad in it. We ask Allah ta'ala to establish this great, discriminating and protecting Istikhara of Sayyiduna Muhammad in our hearts in every situation so that we may pass through the world protected, gaining and giving only good by the mercy and limitless bounty of our Lord.

THE GARDEN OF PRESENCE

Allah, subhanahu wa ta'ala, says in His Noble Book:

$$سَارِعُوٓا۟ إِلَىٰ مَغْفِرَةٍ مِّن رَّبِّكُمْ وَجَنَّةٍ عَرْضُهَا ٱلسَّمَٰوَٰتُ وَٱلْأَرْضُ أُعِدَّتْ لِلْمُتَّقِينَ ۝$$

Race each other to forgiveness from your Lord and a Garden as wide as the heavens and the earth, prepared for the people who have taqwa:

Who are the people who have taqwa?

$$ٱلَّذِينَ يُنفِقُونَ فِى ٱلسَّرَّآءِ وَٱلضَّرَّآءِ$$

those who give in times of both ease and hardship

This is the instruction manual for the human being: give when things are difficult and when things are easy – and you will have forgiveness and a Garden as wide as the heavens and the earth.

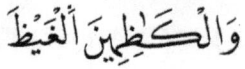

and those who contain their rage

'Ghaydh' is intense anger at some perceived wrong done to you by someone else. 'Kathuma' means to keep silent. 'Kathama' means to repress or keep something under wraps. It is most often used in conjunction with 'ghaydh'.

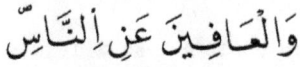

and pardon other people

People will wrong us. We must contain our rage. And we must forgive them.

How do we prevent rage from overcoming us? Rasul, sallallahu 'alayhi wa sallam, said, "Anger is like fire, so when you get angry, do wudu." He also said, sallallahu 'alayhi wa sallam, "If you get angry, sit down. If you are still angry, lie down."

This reflects an elemental understanding of anger as a fire whose flames are fanned by standing and raising up the body. The cure is the opposite element, water, and physically lowering the body.

But this must be followed by forgiveness, because anger that remains becomes rancour, and rancour is poison in the heart.

If you are wronged, and it will not leave you, you must speak, otherwise your anger will turn to rancour. Allah ta'ala says:

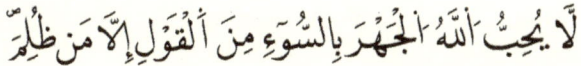

Allah does not like evil words being voiced out loud,
except in the case of someone
who has been wronged.

In the Tafsir of Jalalayn: "...unless a person has been wronged, in which case He would not punish him for speaking out if he is informing others of the wrong done to him by the wrong-doer."

It is not wrong to speak about something that has been done to you, if the intention is to resolve things. If voicing a wrong comes from a place of anger, it will lead to more anger. If it comes from a place of purifying your heart and resolving something that is stuck, then it is not only permitted but sometimes necessary before we can forgive someone. Something has to be said.

After mentioning the containment of rage and pardoning people, Allah ta'ala says:

$$\text{وَٱللَّهُ يُحِبُّ ٱلْمُحْسِنِينَ}$$

Allah loves the Muhsineen.

Controlling rage and forgiving others are actions that make you Muhsin. They are beautiful actions.

He, subhanahu wa ta'ala, continues:

$$\text{وَٱلَّذِينَ إِذَا فَعَلُوا فَاحِشَةً أَوْ ظَلَمُوا أَنفُسَهُمْ}$$

those who, when they act indecently
or wrong themselves

– So the people of taqwa are not people who do not do these things. They are those who, when they do them –

$$\text{ذَكَرُوا ٱللَّهَ فَٱسْتَغْفَرُوا لِذُنُوبِهِمْ}$$

remember Allah and ask forgiveness
for their bad actions.

The ayat continues:

$$\text{وَمَن يَغْفِرُ ٱلذُّنُوبَ إِلَّا ٱللَّهُ وَلَمْ يُصِرُّوا عَلَىٰ مَا فَعَلُوا وَهُمْ يَعْلَمُونَ ۝ أُوْلَٰئِكَ جَزَاؤُهُم مَّغْفِرَةٌ مِّن رَّبِّهِمْ وَجَنَّاتٌ تَجْرِي مِن تَحْتِهَا ٱلْأَنْهَارُ خَالِدِينَ فِيهَا}$$

(and who can forgive bad actions except Allah?) and do not knowingly persist in what they were doing. Their recompense is forgiveness from their Lord, and Gardens with rivers flowing under them, remaining in them timelessly, for ever.

This is the Garden which, as Allah ta'ala says, is:

prepared – made ready

In other words, it already exists and is present.

Qadi 'Iyad emphasises this when he says that one of the obligations of belief is to believe:

"That the Garden and the Fire are real. That they are both in existence, prepared for the people of misery and the people of happiness."

What is it that earns us the Garden that already exists and is present? Allah, subhanahu wa ta'ala, says in Surat al-Baqara:

وَٱلْمُوفُونَ بِعَهْدِهِمْ إِذَا عَٰهَدُوا۟
وَٱلصَّٰبِرِينَ فِى ٱلْبَأْسَآءِ وَٱلضَّرَّآءِ وَحِينَ ٱلْبَأْسِ
أُو۟لَٰٓئِكَ ٱلَّذِينَ صَدَقُوا۟

> those who honour their agreements
> when they make them,
> and are steadfast in poverty and illness and in battle.
> Those are the people who are true.

They are the people of Sidq. Shaykh 'Abdalqadir as-Sufi says about the 'Sadiqun' in his Hundred Steps: "The people of Sidq have a perfume that is not of cleanliness or scents, but directly from the Garden of the Presence." The Garden *is* Presence. The Garden is not confined by time, it is "timelessly, forever". Therefore it is never out of existence. It is present.

Allah says that when they are given fruit there as provision –

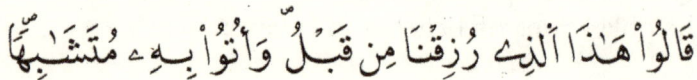

> they will say, 'This is what we were given before.'
> But they were only given a simulation of it.

The kuffar, reflecting their inner condition, claim that this world is where everything is, or should be, possible, and that once you are dead you become nothing and absent. The opposite is true. This world is the realm of limits and duty. Not duty in the depressing puritanical sense, but duty in the sense of what would you not do for someone you love? And this world is the world of semblance – mutashabiha – and illusion. Not illusion in the nihilistic sense that it does not matter. Illusion in the sense that the things of this world are here to show you what awaits you. The Akhira is the realm of limitlessness and reality.

The Garden is

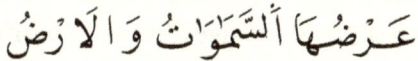

as wide as the heavens and the earth

because not only is time finished, so too are the spatial dimensions.

From Abu Saeed al-Khudri: the Prophet said, "In the Garden, there is a tree that it would take the rider of a swift horse one hundred years to get past." There are other well-known descriptions of the fruit of the garden being of a size which it is impossible to comprehend. The features of the Garden do not have a size in the way we understand.

The Garden is present, not bounded by time or space.

* * *

If you wish for your children and their children to have the safety of the Deen, then it is not enough to do only the obligatory things, although as our Messenger said, doing them will guarantee you the Garden – and Allah knows the judgment on people.

But be warned of a world in which nothing is obligatory for us any more. A world in which there is not enough money left over, so we do not need to give sadaqa. A world in which we have fallen for so many debts and mortgages and credit cards that offset our savings, we are no longer obliged to give Zakat. A world in which corporate interests have so captured hospitality, that Hajj has become too expensive and we no longer have to go, or in which the state has captured our duties so comprehensively that it decides when we go on Hajj.

It is not enough to look to our own families and our own community. We must look beyond them and serve others. I warn you, by Allah, to expand and grow.

I order you, with the permission of Allah, to establish the five prayers.

I call you, by Allah, to the Garden of Presence which is never absent and is always there.

www.ingramcontent.com/pod-product-compliance
Lightning Source LLC
Chambersburg PA
CBHW021844090426
42811CB00033B/2132/J